"I've had the privilege of witnessing [...] the time they occurred, but reading them all together has taken my belief in God's faithfulness to another level. Pastor Edward's simple "yes" to God's call made way for 30 uniquely impactful stories to be strung together in such a way that only God could've authored it. I have no doubt that after you read through these stories, you will be encouraged in your calling, assured of God's power, and compelled to walk through your next step of obedience."

—Lanae Romero,
Original Core Team Member,
Oakland, California

"Edward Paz is a gifted communicator who is passionate about Christ and his church. This book celebrates what God has done and gives hope that God can do miracles in and through your life, too."

—Paul McGovern,
Founding/Lead Pastor,
Crossroads Church, Fremont, California

"If you have thought about or are thinking about church planting, you won't want to miss this book. Edward has a particular gift for looking backward and forward with the deep reflections from which spiritual growth emerges. He traces times of despair and breakthrough, self-doubt and encouragement, obstacles and open doors in ways that weave together his story that God is writing. In the midst of this is a story of partnership where there might have been competition that gives us a glimpse of God's kingdom right here in Oakland."

—Nancy Ortberg,
Chief Executive Officer,
Transforming the Bay with Christ

"The beauty of this book is not that it inspires you to expect God to work in your life the same way he worked in these stories. Rather, Edward points us to the character of God. Our unchanging Lord is ready to reveal himself to you today to transform your life, family, ministry, and work."

—Daniel Henderson,
President,
Strategic Renewal International

"Starting a church is one of the most challenging things a person could ever do. Money is often inadequate. Volunteers can be scarce. Feelings can get hurt. Relationships can be broken. But starting a church can also be the most incredible thing a person could ever do. People give their lives to Jesus. Relationships are restored. Communities are served. Lives are transformed. Edward's account of God's work through THEMOVEMENT.CHURCH so far includes accounts of all of the above and more. It is a great record to have and a great foundation upon which to build."

—**Kevin Ezell,**
President,
North American Mission Board, SBC

"If you enjoy hearing testimonies of God working miraculously in the lives of individuals and the church, you will love *Only God*. What a blessing to have had a front-row seat to witness this powerful story firsthand. Edward—thanks for sharing about the journey."

—**Ricky Wheeler,**
Executive Pastor, Global Ministry,
Johnson Ferry Baptist Church, Marietta, Georgia

"In today's social climate, authenticity and transparency are the bookends of healthy relational connections. In this firsthand account of trusting God even when it logically makes no sense, Pastor Edward Paz does a masterful job of telling the story of the church he planted while offering a crystal clear framework to understanding why healthy relational connections provide the groundswell necessary for a move of God. If you've got any entrepreneurial aspirations whatsoever, read this book and allow it to encourage you to take that first step!"

—**Malcolm Marshall,**
Campus Pastor, Houston's First Baptist Church – Sienna,
Houston Rockets Lead Chaplain

"Edward Paz's book *Only God* is a moving testimony of God's faithfulness to Edward and the people at THEMOVEMENT.CHURCH in Oakland, California. Christian leaders and church planters will be encouraged as they read story after story, the good and the bad, and see how only God can plant a church. I loved it!"

—**Nick Parsons,**
Recruitment Director,
Orchard Group

"Church planting is ministry on the front lines of war—not war against flesh and blood, but war against various spiritual oppositions and antagonists. As such, planting couples experience a myriad of struggles and challenges unique to their calling. They're also given an opportunity to see with fresh eyes the joy of God's provision and the power of his Spirit. Edward Paz's book gives you an opportunity to see both in the birth and growth of THEMOVEMENT.CHURCH. If you are exploring God's calling on your life to church planting, read this book and allow the Lord to continue to shape your heart and mind through this transparent account of Paz's joys and challenges in planting THEMOVEMENT.CHURCH."

—**Micah Millican,**
Senior Director of Planter Development,
Send Network

"I have been around hundreds of church planters over the last 20 years. Every once in a while God gives a young leader the skills, character, and vision of Edward Paz. *Only God* is a must-read primer for anyone considering church planting. Furthermore, it's a great book for anyone who has stopped believing that God is working and expanding his kingdom through the local church."

—**Shaun Garman,**
Associate Director,
Acts 29 US West

ONLY

A SUPERNATURAL CHURCH-PLANTING STORY

GOD

EDWARD PAZ

LUCIDBOOKS

Only God
A Supernatural Church-Planting Story

Copyright © 2020 by Edward Paz

Published by Lucid Books in Houston, TX
www.LucidBooksPublishing.com

ISBN-13: 978-1-63296-495-3
eISBN-13: 978-1-63296-891-3

Special Sales: Most Lucid Books titles are available in special quantity discounts. Custom imprinting or excerpting can also be done to fit special needs. Contact Lucid Books at Info@LucidBooksPublishing.com.

To the many churches that believed and invested in the vision of THEMOVEMENT.CHURCH before there was any evidence of its validity—thank you. In those early years, your faith in what God could do through our church increased my faith to believe he could actually do it!

Sending Church

Crossroads Church (Fremont, California)

Partner Churches

Echo.Church (San Jose, California)
Epic Church (San Francisco, California)
The Bridge Foursquare Church (Foster City, California)
Good News Fellowship (Daly City, California)

Johnson Ferry Baptist Church (Marietta, Georgia)
Central Baptist Church (Warner Robins, Georgia)

Houston's First Baptist Church (Houston, Texas)
Southcliff Baptist Church (Fort Worth, Texas)
Stonegate Fellowship (Midland, Texas)

First Baptist Church Trussville (Trussville, Alabama)
Shades Mountain Baptist Church (Birmingham, Alabama)
Liberty Baptist Church (Chelsea, Alabama)

Cason Foundation (Fredericksburg, Virginia)

Denominational Partners

North American Mission Board (SEND Network)
California State Baptist Convention
East Bay Baptist Association

Table of Contents

Year Three (2015–2016)

Year Four (2016–2017)

Year Five (2017–2018)

Foreword

He is before all things, and in him all things hold together.

—Col. 1:17

God called Jacob, Moses, and Joshua to build altars at times, not for burnt offerings or sacrifice but for remembering the specific times when he showed himself faithful, merciful, loving, powerful, just, and forgiving—to help his people remember when he showed himself to be God. The altars served as remembrances not only for these leaders but also for generations to come so that all who follow God could praise him for centuries.

Too often, we experience God's hand moving in our lives and our churches and then continue without ever looking back to see how God orchestrated our steps all along. By neglecting retrospection, we miss out on the joys of realizing that God is always in control and present in both the good and the seemingly bad circumstances we endure.

I have been privileged to see the story of THEMOVEMENT.CHURCH in Oakland, California, unfold and to see the Lord lead Edward Paz in loving a city, planting a church, and expanding God's kingdom. Edward has wisely kept record of God's movement along the way and shares it unfiltered and honestly. As I read about THEMOVEMENT.CHURCH, I cannot help but think back on the ways I have seen God move in my church. At Johnson Ferry, we have placed memorial plaques at key points around our facility so that people will know and remember those times when God did something miraculous and historic in our midst—something only he could do. What a joy to be reminded of God's unique and astonishing work in my own life!

While this is the origin story of just one church, it is also a celebration of what God is doing through faithful people, following him across our country and the world. We rejoice in the miraculous, knowing that miracles are not unique. God is constantly performing them. He is constantly creating stories just like the ones recounted in this book.

I pray that the story of THEMOVEMENT.CHURCH, led by one of the finest church planters we have partnered with, will encourage you to recount and celebrate the times in your own life and church when the single explanation is. . . Only God.

Bryant Wright
Founding Pastor, Johnson Ferry Baptist Church
Past President, Southern Baptist Convention

Introduction

Why This Book?

So, "Put up the stones," says God, so that they will be a reminder, the people will be arrested, they will say, "What are these stones about? What does this mean?" and then the answer will be given to them.

David Martyn Lloyd-Jones, *Revival*

Can forgetting be characterized as sinful? I sure hope not. Though there are many days when I experience the grace, provision, kindness, and mercy of God, there are also many others when I have doubts that God even exists!

I don't want my life to be marked by this type of forgetting. I want my life to be characterized by remembering—remembering God.

Through the first five years of my journey of planting THEMOVEMENT.CHURCH in Oakland, California (and in many of the years prior), I have experienced God do miraculous things—things that only could've occurred if God was involved, his hand was active, and his power was present.

The purpose of this book, then, is to be like the stones for the nation of Israel: a reminder for me and others of what God has done.

1

This isn't a book about what I hoped God would do, prayed God would do, or believed God would do. This is a book about what God *actually* did, and I needed to write it so when I start to forget, I can read this book to remember.

But it's not only the miracles I want to remember. Behind every miracle of God is also an attribute of God that must not be forgotten. The miracles display what God has done; the attributes describe who God is.

Unfortunately, too often we place a greater emphasis on what God has done than on who God is. This misplacement is problematic. Our understanding of who God is cannot be dependent on what God is or isn't doing on our behalf. What God does changes; who God is never changes. God's character isn't derived from his actions; his actions are derived from his character.

This is an important distinction to make because the more we can tether our faith to who God is, the stronger and more immovable our faith will be when we can't understand what he's doing.

Inspiration through God's miracles and revelation through God's attributes—that is what you can look forward to encountering in the pages to follow.

Who Is This Book For?
For THEMOVEMENT.CHURCH. I want to remind those who have experienced these miracles of how good God has been to us. I want to inform those who didn't experience these miracles of how we became the church we are today. I want to inspire *all* of us to believe that because God has worked mightily in and through our church before, he can work mightily in and through our church again.

2

For our church partners. I want to acknowledge and appreciate you. Without you, we would not be the church we are today. I want to share with you some of what God has done in our church so you can celebrate the harvest grown from the seeds you have sown. I want to encourage you to keep investing in church-planting efforts all around the world. Prayerfully, your faith can be increased to believe that church planting is, indeed, the single greatest means for reaching and discipling lost people with the gospel of Jesus Christ.

For church planters and church-planting teams. I want to inspire you. If God can use a college dropout like me to plant a church that proclaims the gospel and makes disciples, he can surely use you. I want to encourage you. The same God who is working in our church is the same God who can work and *is* working miracles in your church, too. I also want to challenge you. Document the miracles that God is performing in your ministry. He is worthy of the praise that will overflow from the gratitude that comes from remembering.

For those interested in a more robust understanding of God. I want to show you God's power and might through the miracles we've experienced. I want to describe to you just some of the endless attributes of God that put him in a class all by himself. I want to convince you that in light of who God is, he is worthy to be trusted with every part of your life.

And how exactly do I intend for this book to connect with such a wide range of people?

Only God.

PRE-LAUNCH YEARS
(2008–2013)

Chapter 1

Three Deaths

He cried out with a loud voice, "Lazarus, come out." The man who had died came out, his hands and feet bound with linen strips, and his face wrapped with a cloth.

—John 11:43–44

My life was a mess. I was a 25-year-old college dropout whose fascination with financial freedom, dedication to success, and desperation for significance got me absolutely nowhere.

My pride and arrogance drove me to recklessly quit the best-paying job I had ever had. I quit to pursue an entrepreneurial endeavor of selling goal-setting programs, but I didn't set a realistic goal of when I would be able to replace the income from my previous employment. How ironic. The job my wife, Rebekah, had became our only steady stream of income. We had no health insurance.

It was bad, but it got worse.

When my entrepreneurial endeavor to sell goal-setting programs didn't make the necessary income we needed soon enough, our two brand-new cars got repossessed, my wife and I got evicted from our apartment, and I was placed on

ChexSystems for writing a $1,000 check I didn't have the money for. I felt humiliated on so many levels.

But even more troubling than my financial struggles was the state of my relationships. In short, all the people in my life were sick of me trying to sell them something. I constantly sold my wife on the idea that things were going to get better and that I was doing "God's will." I constantly sold my family on why my latest endeavor was "the one." I constantly sold my friends on a new product or business venture and why they should join me.

Nobody wanted to be around me because of my nonstop salesmanship. I didn't even want to be around me! I was ashamed, depressed, and out of ideas. Thankfully, this set of circumstances provided the perfect environment for the first, very necessary death to occur.

The First Death

In the midst of my financial and relational struggles, my friend Kwaku gave me a call. Aware of my situation, he lovingly (but sternly) shared a verse that, up to that point, I don't think I even knew about:

> But if anyone does not provide for his relatives, and especially for members of his household, he has denied the faith and is worse than an unbeliever.
>
> —1 Tim. 5:8

I was convicted in the deepest part of my being. Though I wanted to push back and give excuses for how I *was* trying to provide for my family, the bottom line was that I wasn't.

Within weeks, I came to a much-needed conclusion.

I needed to go back to work. My dream of becoming somebody had become a nightmare. It was imperative that I earn a steady paycheck and for my wife and I to have health insurance again. As an indicator of how serious I was about living a "normal" life, I even suggested we stop watching movies and shows solely off the Internet and finally get a TV, like every other "normal" family. Until that point in our marriage, we hadn't had one.

Though we didn't end up getting a TV (we were too broke), I did end up getting a job. I worked at 24 Hour Fitness selling fitness memberships. My previous job paid me close to six figures. At 24 Hour Fitness, I made minimum wage plus commissions. It was the fall of 2009, and there I was back at the very same job I had held five years prior when Rebekah and I first got married. Ego—dead.

The Second Death

On March 1, 2010, after dealing with kidney failure for more than 15 years, my father-in-law passed away. His death was somewhat sudden, so my wife and I rushed to find airline tickets at an affordable price that would take us to my wife's hometown of Sugar Land, Texas.

After securing buddy passes from a relative, we flew standby to Houston to be present with her family and join them for the funeral. Like most people experiencing the loss of a loved one, I found myself contemplating my life. What was my purpose? Was I accomplishing what I had been created for? What would my legacy be?

Because I had to work the following Monday, I could stay in Houston for only a few days. Flying standby, I attempted to catch several flights back home, but because it was the beginning of spring break, all the flights were full. I spent nearly 10 hours in the airport before my wife had to come back to pick me up.

As a result, I was able to attend the 10-year anniversary celebration of my wife's uncle's church on Sunday, March 7, 2010. At an event I never planned to attend, a third death took place, and my future was changed forever.

The Third Death

The service started, as most church anniversary services typically do, with songs, special music, and testimonies. Then, the preaching.

I can't recall what the preacher's message was about, but I do remember that at the end, he invited anyone who wanted to commit his or her life to the Lord by committing to vocational ministry to come forward.

Every head was bowed, and every eye was closed. I felt a knot in the pit of my stomach. In a matter of seconds, the last few years of my life flashed before my eyes—striving, manipulating, excuse-making, and failing. Though I didn't know what a life of vocational ministry would look like, I was tired of doing things my way for my selfish gain.

I stood up, walked forward, and received a powerful prayer. In that moment, God put to death what I had been idolizing and pursuing for far too long—*my* definition of success. By what only can be explained as an act of God, I didn't want what I wanted for my life anymore. For the first time, all I wanted for me was what God wanted for me. Nothing more, nothing less.

Only God could've saved me from an ego that manifested itself in an all-consuming desire for success. Only God could've used my father-in-law's untimely death to orchestrate my attendance at a church service I never was supposed to be at. Only God could've put a desire in my heart to exchange my will for my life for his will for my life.

Only God can take the messiest parts of your past and use them as the raw materials for making a masterpiece of your future.

Only God.

Attribute of God #1 – God Is a Resurrector
Only God can bring life from death.

Questions for Reflection:
1. What needs to die *in* your life so God can do more *through* your life?
2. What do you need to persist in believing God can resurrect?
3. For church planters, church-planting team members, ministry leaders, and volunteers: How might your ego and desire for *your* definition of success be undermining what God desires to do in and through your ministry?

Chapter 2

Crossroads Church

Humble yourselves, therefore, under the mighty hand of God so that at the proper time he may exalt you.

—1 Pet. 5:6

No college degree. No formal theological education. No vocational ministry experience. Typically, churches don't hire guys like me.

Thankfully, Pastor Paul McGovern—founder and lead Pastor of Crossroads Church in Fremont, California, took a chance on me anyway. In August 2010, only five months after responding to God's call on my life into vocational ministry, Pastor Paul hired me to become the church's interim High School Ministry Director.

No striving required. No toiling experienced. No self-promoting imposed. When I was offered the job at Crossroads, for the first time in my life I experienced a sense of peace, satisfaction, and joy that comes from walking through doors that only God could've opened for me.

And it only got better.

Despite my lack of experience and education, God showed favor on the high school ministry, and only four months after

I was hired, my part-time interim title became full-time permanent. (I was also eventually ordained as a pastor.) After several years of stress and instability both financially and vocationally, things were starting to come together.

But as much of a gift as financial and vocational stability was it paled in comparison to the three additional gifts I would receive during my two and a half years at Crossroads Church. Without these three gifts, I have no doubt in my mind that THEMOVEMENT.CHURCH would've never started.

Gift #1 - Experience

As valuable as theological education can be, there is no better preparation *for* ministry than experience *in* ministry. And during my time at Crossroads, I had many rich, life-giving ministry experiences.

First, there were the joyful experiences. I witnessed God bring many people to saving faith by his grace and through the preaching of the gospel. I baptized more than 100 high school students and young adults. I watched lives transformed for the glory of God right before my eyes. I experienced so much celebration, gladness, and victory.

But there were also the sorrowful experiences. I ministered to kids growing up in homes without loving parents. I counseled students struggling with suicidal thoughts and depression. I invested in troubled marriages that ended up choosing divorce. I experienced so much hurt, brokenness, and pain.

In addition to the sorrowful experiences, there were the experiences that taught me that ministry required more emotional energy than it did physical energy. I learned that boldly preaching truths the world rejects, persistently praying for people whose hearts are hardened to the gospel, and unconditionally loving those who ignore your pastoral counsel are exhausting. I experienced so much spiritual warfare.

There were also the experiences of loss. Students I loved moved unexpectedly. Volunteers I appreciated quit suddenly. Others I invested in left the church angrily. I experienced so much relational instability.

On a more positive note, there were the fun experiences, too. There were summer camps, winter camps, mission trips, and crazy all-nighters. But what I found most rewarding was recruiting, leading, and developing a team to accomplish a vision. Who knew planning meetings, debrief meetings, and strategic meetings with a team of volunteers could be so much fun? (At least I thought so!) I experienced so much enjoyment from the leadership aspect of pastoral ministry.

God knew. He knew I needed to experience the ups and downs of pastoral ministry *before* I started a church. He knew that going through these experiences would both prepare me for the work of a church planter and prove to me that this was the type of work I wanted to do for the rest of my life.

But as good as the gift of ministry experience was, the next gift was even better.

Gift #2 - Permission

There were the Cheas, the Prices, and the Romeros—only God could've brought such beautiful couples into my life. In addition to coming alongside me to create and lead one of the most fun, engaging, Jesus-exalting high school ministries in all of Fremont (in my opinion), they gave me a gift that they had no idea I needed—permission.

You see, I had abused many of my previous friendships for selfish gain. So when I first became the High School Ministry Director, not only was I unsure of whether my motivations for leadership had changed, but I was also unsure whether anyone would ever trust me to lead them again. These couples gave me a chance.

They believed in my philosophy of ministry. They enjoyed my style of leadership. They embraced my approach to preaching. Though I was new to vocational ministry, they were encouraging and supportive.

But more than just believing in me as the leader of the ministry they were volunteering for, they also believed in me as their pastor. At a time when I was still discovering who I was as a pastor, they graciously allowed me to pastor them. They asked for my counsel, confessed their sins, received from my preaching, and took difficult steps of obedience. They were the first adults who invited me into their lives and gave me the permission to be their pastor. (Side note: pastoral ministry is best received when permission has first been given.)

These couples were an absolute godsend. If they didn't trust me to pastor them, I would've never believed I could pastor others.

By God's grace, I officiated at two of their weddings and baptized three of them. When I invited all of them to join the Core Team that would go on to start THEMOVEMENT. CHURCH, they all accepted.

Gift #3 – Affirmation

In the past, when it came to transitioning from one job or entrepreneurial endeavor to another, I did so because I was fired or I quit. I rarely, if ever, finished well, and I was definitely never sent away with *affirmation*.

Leaving Crossroads Church was different.

Pastor Paul and the leadership team of the church were not only gracious hiring someone as inexperienced as I was, but they were also generous in the myriad of ways they affirmed me and my team as we made plans to start a new church.

Not only did Pastor Paul privately affirm and approve God's call on my life to start a church, but he also publicly affirmed me. He agreed that Crossroads would be my "sending church." What that meant was that Crossroads would take the primary responsibility for the new church getting a healthy start. They committed to provide funding, they loaned us human resources to keep our books, and they even encouraged the people of Crossroads to join *our* team! Pastor Paul actually went before the entire church of more than 700 people and said that whoever wanted to go with us could go. Never in my life had I received this much affirmation for an endeavor I was pursuing.

This affirmation was most clearly displayed during one of my last weekends at Crossroads Church. In each of the four services, Pastor Paul brought me on stage to thank me for my years of service at Crossroads. He presented me with very thoughtful gifts and then brought my wife and our team forward to pray a prayer of blessing over us. For the first time in my life, I didn't feel as if the success of what I was pursuing depended fully on me.

Being affirmed in this way provided me with unwavering confidence, supernatural covering, and all the comfort I needed to know that what I was doing was God's will and not my own. What a gift!

Only God could've given the gift of experience to someone who wasn't qualified for the experience. Only God could've given the gift of permission to someone who wasn't qualified for the permission. Only God could've given the gift of affirmation to someone who wasn't qualified for the affirmation.

Though the world only calls the qualified, only God can qualify the called.

Only God.

Attribute of God #2 – God Is a Promoter
*Only God can gift you opportunities that
your lack of education and experience should
disqualify you from.*

Questions for Reflection:

1. What areas of your life do you need to trust more in God's power to promote you than in your plans to promote yourself?

2. Who do you need to gift an opportunity to even though that person may not have the necessary education or experience?

3. For church planters, church-planting team members, ministry leaders, and volunteers: When you get impatient with God's timeline of "promotion," how do you default to self-promotion?

Chapter 3

A Change of Plans

"The wall of Jerusalem is broken down, and its gates are destroyed by fire." As soon as I heard these words I sat down and wept and mourned for days, and I continued fasting and praying before the God of heaven.

—Neh. 1:3–4

Our team had every intention of starting our church somewhere in the Silicon Valley of California. In addition to being the technology hub of the world, it was also an area where a few other churches had recently started and seen success. Because the area was filled with so much action, innovation, and influence, we figured it would be a strategic place to begin our ministry. But one conversation and one specific sentence in that conversation changed all our plans.

The Ugly Stepbrother

Just a few months before leaving Crossroads Church, I met with Lyman Alexander, the Director of Missions for the East Bay Baptist Association, to talk about the location of our future church plant. After telling him about our plans to plant in the Silicon Valley, he asked me if I had ever thought about planting a church in Oakland.

I quickly replied, "No, not really."

He went on to tell me about the need for a multiethnic church for young professionals in the city of Oakland. He said there was a need for a church in the Jack London Square area and that the association had been praying for a church planter to start a church there for some time.

I wasn't sold.

After he continued to describe the need for several more minutes, he said, "I don't know if you've ever heard this, but Oakland is seen as the ugly stepbrother of San Francisco."

In that moment, God immediately gave me a burden for the city of Oakland. For some reason, it wasn't okay with me that Oakland had such a negative reputation. Though I had never cared about Oakland before, suddenly I cared.

On the way home from the meeting and for the first time since deciding to plant our church somewhere in the Silicon Valley, I considered that the city was about to change.

I had confirmation of this conviction in an even greater way a few weeks after my conversation with Lyman. As I was describing the need for a new church in Oakland to one of the members of our Core Team, she mentioned that she was just in Oakland the previous week. Someone had told her that "Oakland was the armpit of the Bay Area."

I had heard enough. For reasons I cannot fully understand, after hearing these two very negative, disrespectful views of Oakland, I was convinced that Oakland was the city where we needed to start our church. No longer would the location of our church be based on what was most strategic. Instead, it would be determined by where God was leading and by how God was speaking.

Only God could've used two descriptions *of* a city to redirect me *to* a city I had no intention of going to. Only God could've given me a burden for a city I had no intention of loving. Only God could've moved the hearts of the eight other Core Team members to agree to plans they had no intention of agreeing to.

Only God could've brought his intention to our attention. Only God could've made his desire our duty. Only God could've made his method our mission: *overwhelm Oakland with love.*

Only God can make his purpose your passion.

Only God.

Attribute of God #3 – God Is a Burden-Giver

*Only God can burden your heart for
the things that break his heart.*

Questions for Reflection:

1. What areas of your life are driven more by a man-made strategy than a God-given burden?
2. What burden has God given you for your sphere of influence that you have not acted on?
3. For church planters, church-planting team members, ministry leaders, and volunteers: Are your ministry efforts driven by a God-given burden? If not, why not? If so, what is it?

Chapter 4

Wifey's Approval

The hand of God was also on Judah to give them one heart to do what the king and the princes commanded by the word of the LORD.

—2 Chron. 30:12

My wife wasn't convinced. Though the call to plant a church in the city of Oakland was clear for me and our team, initially, she wasn't on board.

For the first six years of our marriage, I had sold her on many dreams and visions for my life that led to multiple vocational transitions and financial instability. We moved seven times in our first six years of marriage. Being married to me was exhausting.

On top of that, my being the High School Pastor at Crossroads Church gave us a financial stability we hadn't had since we got married. I had a bank account again. We had a car that was paid off. Sure, it was a 1997 Saturn station wagon, but it was paid off. And we both had health insurance.

Why would she agree to leave the most sure and stable situation we had ever been in for something as unsure and unstable as starting a church, from scratch, in a city we had never lived in? Thankfully, she ended up reading a book that became the catalyst for her taking a huge step of faith—following my lead one more time.

Sun Stand Still

I'll never forget the day. My wife said she wanted to take me to breakfast because she had something important to tell me. When we sat down at Posh Bagel in Fremont, she told me to mark down the date and time because what she had to say was *big*. With bagel dog in hand (I love bagel dogs), I anticipated what she would say next.

She proceeded to tell me she had read Steven Furtick's book *Sun Stand Still*—a book about audacious faith and following God regardless of the cost. She said God had convicted her, and she didn't want to miss out on what God had for our lives.

Then she told me, very pointedly, "I'm giving you permission to plant this church."

She knew our lives would be drastically impacted. She knew our marriage would pay a price. She knew our future would be dramatically changed. But God had spoken very clearly to her, and she was ready to obey.

Having the approval and affirmation of Pastor Paul and Crossroads Church was encouraging, but having the approval and affirmation of my wife was *necessary*. Could I really expect God to bless my ministry in the church if I wasn't prioritizing the unity in my marriage?

Only God could've convinced my wife that planting a church was his will for our lives. Only God could've given my wife the courage to follow me despite my past failures. Only God, by the power of his Holy Spirit, could've compelled my wife to willingly exchange security for the unknown.

Only God can unify a marriage within a calling to ministry. Only God.

Attribute of God #4 – God Is a Unifier

*Only God can develop relational unity around a
calling that will require that the
relationship pay a price.*

Questions for Reflection:

1. What relationships impacted by your calling do you need to trust God to unify?

2. Whose calling is God requiring you to be more supportive of and on board with?

3. For church planters, church-planting team members, ministry leaders, and volunteers: How are you pursuing relational unity in the relationships impacted by your calling?

YEAR ONE
(2013–2014)

Chapter 5

Arrival

And behold the divisions of the priests and the Levites for all the service of the house of God; and with you in all the work will be every willing man who has skill for any kind of service.

—1 Chron. 28:21

My wife and I moved to Oakland in January 2013. Here was the plan for launching the church:

- Core Team members would relocate to Oakland as soon as they could find housing.
- My employment at Crossroads Church would officially end March 31.
- Preview (practice) services would be held once a month in June, July, and August to develop interest and set us up to launch with a critical mass of attendees.
- Launch Sunday would be September 15, and weekly services would begin after that.

Though our excitement and passion were high and our timeline had been mapped out, we were lacking a lot of things to be sufficiently prepared to launch in nine months.

We lacked spiritual maturity. The average age of our team was 25 years old, and half of them were relatively new believers. Could a team this new to faith effectively reach a city with the gospel?

We lacked finances. We had a $190,000 pre-launch budget to pay for the start-up costs and salaries from April 2013 to August 2013. By January 2013, we had only secured $20,000. Could a team this underfunded realistically raise enough money in time?

We lacked connections. Most of the people we knew and the churches we had connections to did not have the giving capacity to help us fund our pre-launch budget. Could a team with this limited of a network eventually make enough connections to launch a church with adequate resources?

Thank God he had an absolute gift in store for us upon our arrival in Oakland—the Johnstones.

The Johnstones

I met Rich and Rhonda Johnstone for the first time at Crossroads Church. Toward the end of my time there, they happened to attend a service when I had preached, and they introduced themselves to me when the service ended.

Rich introduced himself as the Bay Area Send City Coordinator for the North American Mission Board (NAMB). I later learned that he had been hired by NAMB—the Church Planting Agency for the Southern Baptist Convention (SBC)—to lead the church-planting mobilization strategy in the Bay Area.

His job entailed encouraging church planters to come to the Bay Area and encouraging churches in other parts of the country to invest their mission dollars to fund church planting there.

For the work we were embarking on, Rich was a great guy to know. Thankfully, just knowing him wasn't where this story would end.

Joining the Team

Unbeknownst to me, Rich, Rhonda, and their daughter Eryn lived one block away from the condo where my wife and I had just moved in the Jack London Square area of Oakland.

After finding out we were planting our church in the city they had just moved to, in the exact neighborhood where they were living, the Johnstones asked if they could be part of our Core Team.

Although Rich's job required him to encourage and resource *all* the church planters in the Bay Area associated with the SBC, he wanted his family to be members of *our* church.

I quickly said, "Of course!"

God would providentially use this family to provide much of what our team lacked and so much more. As a pastor himself, Rich helped me pastor our Core Team and also kept me encouraged and on track as a young church planter. Rich and Rhonda, parents of adult children, mentored and supported the young families on our Core Team. As the Bay Area Send City Coordinator, Rich connected me with tens of thousands of dollars from NAMB to help with the start-up costs of the church plant.

Only God could've orchestrated our meeting at Crossroads just months before we planted a church. Only God could've arranged for us to live less than a quarter of a mile away from the Johnstones in the exact neighborhood we intended to plant our church. Only God could've moved on the hearts of a family so spiritually mature and experienced in ministry to join such a young team.

Only God can bring just the right people into your life at exactly the right time to accomplish specifically what he intends to do.

Only God.

Attribute of God #5 – God Is an Equipper
Only God can call people who are overqualified
to follow you to commit to your vision.

Questions for Reflection:
1. What providential relationships do you need to express gratitude and appreciation for?
2. In whose life may you need to be a providential relationship?
3. For church planters, church-planting team members, ministry leaders, and volunteers: What team member do you need to persist in believing that God will eventually equip you with?

Chapter 6

One Million Dollars

Then the Lord said to Moses, "I will rain down bread from heaven for you."

—Exod. 16:4 NIV

On February 19, 2013, I received the opportunity of a lifetime.

About 40 church leaders (many of them missions pastors) representing 20 or so churches had flown out from various churches in the South (many of them megachurches) for a Catch the Vision Tour. The tour was organized by Rich Johnstone (the gift that keeps on giving) and Bryant Wright, the Senior Pastor and Founder of Johnson Ferry Baptist Church in Marietta, Georgia, and a past president of the SBC. It gave several church planters in the Bay Area the opportunity to share their visions for their churches in front of a group of pastors who already had interest in financially supporting church planting there. (If you know anything about sales, this was the epitome of what would be defined as a "qualified lead.")

This was a church planter's dream!

20 Minutes I Will Never Forget

All 40 of these church leaders ended up cramming into our small two-bedroom condo, where I shared the vision of our church. The church I envisioned:

- Passionately preached the gospel
- Relentlessly reached the lost
- Deliberately developed disciples
- Strategically served the city
- Methodically multiplied itself

This was the church I saw, and this was the church I believed we would become.

When I finished, Pastor Paul McGovern confirmed to the men and women in the room that our vision for our church was one worth investing in. In my opinion, his affirming words were the most compelling part of the presentation. (Once again, Pastor Paul showed himself to be one of the most kingdom-minded pastors I will ever have the privilege of knowing.)

I answered a few questions. Pastor Bryant Wright prayed for Pastor Paul and me. We passed out a one-page handout summarizing our vision and detailing how the churches could get involved. Everyone left. Then, we waited.

Windfall

And God acted.

Because of the Catch the Vision Tour, we developed a partnership with 14 churches by June 2013. We raised our entire launch budget of $190,000, not in future commitments but in cash. Some churches gave one-time donations; others committed for a longer period of time.

One church committed to give us $250,000 over the next four years. Another church committed to give us $75,000 over the next three years. Another church, which had existed for more than 50 years and had never given a dime directly to a church plant, is still giving us $200 a month to this day.

Because of the grace and favor of God and the generosity of so many congregations across the country who believe in church planting, we received more than $1 million in the first five years to support the work of THEMOVEMENT. CHURCH in Oakland, California.

Only God could've aligned the timeline of our church plant with the date of the Catch the Vision Tour. Only God could've been stirring up a burden in the hearts of these pastors for church planting in the Bay Area. Only God could've placed the faith in the pastors of these churches to support someone as inexperienced and uneducated as I was.

Only God can provide for his purposes when you are not positioned to pay for them.

Only God.

Attribute of God #6 – God Is a Provider
Only God can prepare and position people you don't know to bring financial provision into your vision.

Questions for Reflection:
1. Who are the people God has used to bring financial provision into your life? How can you express gratitude and appreciation for them?
2. Who may God be preparing you to be a means of financial provision for?
3. For church planters, church-planting team members, ministry leaders, and volunteers: How can you make yourself more aware of and grateful for how God has financially provided for your ministry as opposed to how he has yet to financially provide for your ministry?

(See Appendix 2, "The Church I See," to read the original vision description I wrote for our church.)

Chapter 7

Leah

If you ask me anything in my name, I will do it.

—John 14:14

With a majority of the Core Team relocated to Oakland and with the finances fully raised to get our church off the ground, we were ready to host our very first public service.

To invite people in Oakland to our first service, we sent out 20,000 mailers to the zip codes surrounding Jack London Square. (Praise God for a fully raised launch budget because mailers aren't cheap.)

About 250 people attended our first service, and only about 20 of them came as a result of the mailers. Only a handful of those people are still at our church today, but I will never regret paying so much money for that particular type of marketing.

On Sunday, June 23, 2013, we met Leah Jordan.

God Heard Her. . .Twice

Leah grew up in Oakland in tough circumstances. Her father struggled with drug addiction. Her mom did the best she could to provide for Leah and her three siblings, but surrounded by drugs and gang violence, life wasn't easy.

When she was just 16 years old, Leah felt such a sense of worthlessness and purposelessness that she attempted to take her life.

As she was getting light-headed from losing so much blood from cutting her wrists, she cried out to the Lord to save her. She told God that if he would spare her life, she would spend the rest of her life serving him.

God heard her cry.

She survived her attempted suicide and began a relationship with the Lord. She began going to church, reading the Bible, and encouraging her family to do the same.

Her family attended church together for a few years, but in the years leading up to the launch of our church, they found themselves disconnected from a church community. They were also struggling with their father's recent imprisonment.

A couple weeks before our first service, Leah was prompted by the Holy Spirit to gather her family together to pray that God would lead them to a community of faith where they could involve themselves.

Again, God heard her cry.

The very next day after praying that prayer, a mailer arrived inviting her family to our service.

Leah has since been baptized, played an integral part in our kids' ministry, and become a prayer warrior who never ceases to pray for the Holy Spirit of God to move powerfully in our church community. Her presence in, contribution toward, and impact on our church over the last five years is immeasurable.

Only God could've intervened during Leah's attempted suicide. Only God could've ordained that a mailer would arrive in Leah's mailbox inviting her to our church service just one day after she gathered with her family to pray for a church. Only God could've heard Leah's prayers and answered.

Only God can prompt us to pray prayers he intends to answer.

Only God.

Attribute of God #7 – God Is a Prayer-Answerer

Only God can answer your prayers supernaturally.

Questions for Reflection:

1. What prayers has God answered that you need to express gratitude and appreciation for?
2. What prayers have you stopped praying that you need to start praying again?
3. For church planters, church-planting team members, ministry leaders, and volunteers: What prayers is God currently prompting you to pray?

Chapter 8

Mills College

Behold, I have set before you an open door, which no one is able to shut.

—Rev. 3:8

Though our first service went well, the location was not a viable option for future services.

Because it was a venue that we rented from the Oakland Parks and Recreation Department, it didn't allow for money to be collected on site. (For those of you who know how churches are financed, that's a major problem.)

Because we intended to send out another mailer inviting people to our July preview service, we were under a lot of pressure to find a new location as soon as possible.

Here we were with yet another major problem. But true to form, God came through with another miraculous solution.

Sandy

After checking out various high schools, junior colleges, private spaces, and other potential meeting places, we found ourselves on the beautiful campus of Mills College in the Millsmont area of Oakland.

Because it was a private university and under no obligation to rent to us (as many publicly owned facilities are), I was very skeptical about Mills allowing us to hold our Sunday services in their auditorium.

I was also hesitant about meeting at Mills because even if they did agree to rent to us, it would take us away from the Jack London Square area of Oakland where we had been preparing for and planning to start our church community.

But then we met Sandy. She was in charge of booking events and room rentals at Mills, and she was also a believer in Jesus Christ.

When she found out we were starting a church, not only was she open to renting us the space, she was ecstatic. She was excited that we were starting a church on a college campus where many faculty members and students were hostile to the gospel.

Even though our original plan wasn't to meet in this neighborhood of Oakland, we definitely sensed that God was leading us to Mills College. Through Sandy's connection, Mills College became the location of our Sunday services, membership gatherings, and special events for the first three and a half years of our ministry.

Only God could've led us to look at a location where a believer in Jesus Christ was in charge of booking room rentals. Only God could've opened the doors for an evangelical church to have its Sunday services on one of the most liberal college campuses in the entire Bay Area. Only God could've made it possible for Lisser Hall on the campus of Mills College to be the site where people would experience and encounter the scandalous love of Jesus Christ for more than three years.

Only God can cause his love to be experienced where it is undesired to be expressed.

Only God.

Attribute of God #8 – God Is a Door-Opener

Only God can position you to be received
where most are rejected.

Questions for Reflection:

1. What doors has God opened for you that you need to express gratitude and appreciation for?

2. What doors do you need to persist in believing that God will open for you?

3. For church planters, church-planting team members, ministry leaders, and volunteers: What ministry opportunities are you neglecting to pursue because you assume you will be rejected?

Chapter 9

Owen

Salvation belongs to the LORD.

—Ps. 3:8

The story of the first salvation at our church is one of my favorites.

One of the first-time guests at our July preview service (our first at Mills College) was Owen. He was a non-Christian, young professional who worked at Shutterfly in the Silicon Valley. After being intrigued by the content of the message during the service, he requested to have a one-on-one meeting with me. We didn't have the meeting until August 16, 2013, at a Starbucks in Hayward, California, but it was a day I will never forget.

In our conversation, we discussed topics such as football (he is originally from Seattle and a huge Seahawks fan), dinosaurs (he wanted to know my thoughts on their existence), Adam and Eve (he was curious if they really were how humanity began), and various other questions about Jesus and faith.

Eventually, I shared the gospel—the good news that Jesus saves sinners—and then asked, "Do you believe this?"

In true Millennial fashion, he replied, "Can I *text* you later when I am ready to make a decision on what I believe?"

At this point in the conversation, I had a critical decision to make. I could twist his arm by asking him, "What if you get hit by a car when you leave here tonight and die? Do you know where you would spend eternity?" or I could trust in the Holy Spirit of God to reveal himself to this young man when the time was right. By God's grace, I chose the latter.

I made this choice because from the very beginning, I wanted our church to be marked by the supernatural power of God, not by people's manipulating ways.

Although he was not ready to put his faith in Christ, we continued our conversation. After moving from inside of Starbucks to outside, I continued to answer his questions the best I could and explain the benefits of Christ's life, death, and resurrection on our behalf.

Then, less than an hour after letting me know that he wanted to text me his decision *later*, he looked at me with tears in his eyes and emphatically said, "I want to place my faith in Jesus Christ *now*."

I was stunned. No arm-twisting was needed. No scare tactics were required. No ridiculous promises of a prosperous future were made. When God decided it was time for Owen to believe in him as Savior and Lord, there was nothing Owen could do to stop it.

That day, I learned a very important lesson that I hope to never forget.

A Ministry Lesson Worth Remembering

Only God can save a soul from eternal separation from him.

Well-articulated sermons can't save a soul.

Relevant, engaging Sunday services can't save a soul.

Altar calls can't save a soul.

Manipulation and coercion can't save a soul.

Friendship can't save a soul.

Church attendance can't save a soul.

Good works can't save a soul.

Moral behavior can't save a soul.

Generosity can't save a soul.

God alone, through the power of the Holy Spirit alone, by the blood of Jesus Christ alone, is the only one who can take a heart hardened by sin and soften it to the point where someone actually decides to repent of their sin and follow him.

Only God.

Launch Sunday

September 15, 2013, was the official launch Sunday of our church.

The service was incredible. Lisser Hall was filled with people. Praises unto God were sung. The gospel was preached. Owen was baptized! And afterward, delicious tacos were served.

A church had been birthed!

It's amazing to think that just a little more than three years before, at the end of a church service in the middle of Texas, I found myself responding to God's call on my life into vocational ministry. Little did I know that in such a short amount of time I would be part of starting a brand-new church in Oakland, California.

A Fruitful First Year

That exciting, God-exalting, fun launch Sunday really set the tone for our entire first year of ministry. We saw our church grow from 20 adults on the Core Team to an average Sunday attendance of more than 100 adults and kids. We saw many people give their lives to Christ and go public with their faith through baptism. We saw people go from strangers to friends to family. We saw missions teams from our partner churches come and serve alongside us in our city. We saw our efforts to serve our city have a positive impact on both our church family and the community.

We saw God move mightily, and we experienced a taste of becoming the movement we prayed we would one day become.

Then, during our one-year anniversary service in September 2014, Owen shared, live from the stage, a testimony of all that God had done in and through his life in the previous year. (He had come such a long way from his days of asking questions about dinosaurs.) God didn't just save Owen through our ministry; he was *sanctifying* Owen as well. (That meant God was making Owen more like him.)

Only God could've predetermined the events that would lead to Owen attending our preview service in July. Only God could've saved Owen by his Spirit. Only God could've transformed Owen more into his image by his grace.

Only God could've carried our young, inexperienced team through our first year together in ministry. Only God could've taken attendees of a service and then transformed them into a family on mission. Only God could've used a small, start-up church like ours to begin making a difference in Oakland.

Only God can rescue sinners and use them as instruments in his hands to rescue more sinners.

Only God.

Attribute of God #9 – God Is a Rescuer
Only God can save a soul.

Questions for Reflection:

1. If you have not yet placed your faith in Jesus Christ for salvation, by what means do you believe your soul can be saved from eternal separation from God?

2. If you have placed your faith in Jesus Christ for salvation, in what ways can you express gratitude and appreciation for God choosing to rescue you?

3. For church planters, church-planting team members, ministry leaders, and volunteers: What are you relying on (possibly unintentionally) other than the power of God to save and sanctify the people you are ministering to?

YEAR TWO
(2014–2015)

Chapter 10

Disaster

I am the true vine, and my Father is the gardener. He cuts off every branch in me that bears no fruit, while every branch that does bear fruit he prunes so that it will be even more fruitful.

—John 15:1–2 NIV

By far, this will be the hardest chapter of our church's short history to write. Because of the fruitfulness of our first year, what happened during our second year was something I would have never dreamed could happen.

Before we could even make it to our second anniversary, the executive pastor of our church and I had a relational breakdown that we would not recover from.

The breakdown began when, during a conversation in his backyard, he admitted to me that he had been speaking poorly of my leadership behind my back in conversations with other key leaders of the church. Though I was surprised and hurt to find this out, he confessed and apologized. I was thankful, and I accepted his apology.

I forgave him completely, but for us to move forward in a healthy way, I also wanted him to confess his wrongdoing and apologize to the key leaders to whom he had been undermining my leadership. Unfortunately, he refused to do so and became angry that I would require this of him.

After attempting to settle these differences on our own, we brought in Rich Johnstone to help facilitate reconciliation. To my disappointment, after one lengthy meeting with the three of us and then one more conversation between the two of us, reconciliation hadn't taken place. He was convinced there was no need for him to publicly confess and apologize. I would later learn that reconciliation isn't possible where repentance isn't present.

After receiving counsel from two of our pastors and two pastors from one of our partner churches, I gave our executive pastor an ultimatum in one last effort to get us back on track. He could either agree to a developmental plan for both his work and our relationship that our pastoral team would oversee, or he could quit and be given a severance.

In May 2013, after dismissing himself and his wife from a very emotional pastoral team meeting, he quit.

Grief

The months and years that followed could be summarized in one word, *grief*—grief for how the situation ended our relationship, grief for how it impacted his family, and grief for how my relationships with other individuals on the Core Team and in the church were never the same.

I grieved for the people's confusion both inside and outside the church who would never understand the full story, for the dozen or so people who left the church in the months that followed, and for the negative impact on the church in general.

But let me not paint myself or the church as merely victims in this situation.

I also grieved that my poor leadership and management were part of the reason things turned out the way they did. I hadn't set clear expectations for the role of executive pastor, and I didn't always follow through or hold him accountable for the expectations I did have. I didn't always privately and publicly appreciate all the work he did behind the scenes, and I didn't set clear boundaries between being his friend and being his boss.

Because of this lack of clarity, when it came time for me to put the "boss hat" on, I could totally see how my requirement of public apology and adherence to a developmental plan could be perceived as blindsiding and unreasonable.

For a long time following the incident, I lived with the grief that came from wondering this: If I had been a better leader, would this still have taken place?

Self-Doubt

This grief then turned into an intense self-doubt.

Did I do everything I could do to live peaceably with him? Were my own apologies for how I had sinned against him thorough enough? Were the ways in which I perceived that he had sinned against me accurate? Was the ultimatum I gave him unfair? Was I delusional?

Questioning myself and how I handled the situation caused me to question everything else, too. How could I expect to lead others well if I couldn't lead my right-hand guy well? How would my reputation remain intact if people believed his version of how the situation unfolded? How would our church recover from the loss of our executive pastor and secondary preaching pastor?

How would I ever restore the relationships with the other people I loved who were negatively impacted by the events? How would our pastoral team maintain unity in leading our church forward? How would our church partners maintain faith in me and our ability to accomplish our mission after such a horrible situation?

How could I ever trust anyone again? How could I protect my wife from ever having to go through something like this with me again? How would I ever get the confidence to pastor again?

Only God could've comforted me as I grieved. Only God could've encouraged me in the midst of my self-doubt. Only God could've convicted me to persist in pastoral ministry despite such a painful experience.

Only God could've known that this situation would form me into a better leader and pastor. Only God could've seen that this situation would develop our church into a stronger community of faith. Only God could've planned for this situation to pave the way for the more fruitful seasons that were to come.

Only God can leverage betrayal as a method of building his church.

Only God.

Attribute of God #10 – God Is a Pruner
Only God can employ subtraction as
a means of multiplication.

Questions for Reflection:

1. What relationships has God removed from your life that you are thankful that he did?
2. What relationships do you need to accept that God may be currently pruning from you?
3. For church planters, church-planting team members, ministry leaders, and volunteers: What proactive steps can you take to prevent betrayal or limit the amount of betrayal you may experience in ministry?

Chapter 11

Recovery

Pray earnestly to the Lord of the harvest to send out laborers into his harvest.

—Matt. 9:38

As the old adage states, "The show must go on."

There were still services to hold, sermons to preach, and small groups to lead. The members of the church still needed to be cared for, and the city still needed to hear the good news. I still needed to lead.

In the months that followed the disaster, I was amazed as I witnessed person after person step up to fill the void left by our former executive pastor and the handful of people who left our church as a result of our unfortunate situation.

Unexpected people stepped up to volunteer sacrificially on Sundays, during service projects, and behind the scenes. God was faithful to provide laborers for every work of the church that needed to continue.

Unexpected people stepped up financially so every bill was paid, every ministry was funded, and every commitment to support other ministries was fulfilled.

Then, by the grace and goodness of God, there were two unexpected people who stepped up and wholeheartedly gave their lives to the mission.

Seminarians to the Rescue

Bekah and Brook. They had graduated from seminary. They lived in and loved the city of Oakland. They were looking for a new church to join and serve in. Could a church planter still licking his wounds from a very painful experience ask for anything more?

They loved Jesus and the mission of our church, and despite my recent leadership struggles, they were still eager to join the team. These two gifts from God not only encouraged me that God wasn't finished with our church, but they also reminded me that God wasn't done with me.

They listened. They prayed. They gave. They served in big tasks, small tasks, onstage, and off. Their level of engagement and commitment was a breath of fresh air that was contagious.

By our two-year church anniversary, just three and a half months after the disaster, they were both serving in leadership positions.

Our leadership team was strengthened. My faith was renewed. Our community of faith had bounced back. The resiliency of the church was obvious, and these words from Jesus Christ that I had been aware of for so long were real to me in a way that they had never been before:

I will build my church, and the gates of hell shall not prevail against it.

—Matt. 16:18

Only God could've sent reinforcements of such a high caliber. Only God could've sent workers who were willing to serve him at a personal cost to themselves. Only God could've sent laborers who were just as eager as I was to overwhelm Oakland with love.

Only God can send saints who would rather serve than settle for merely sitting and consuming religious goods and services.

Only God.

Attribute of God #11 – God Is a Labor-Sender
*Only God can send people to help you rebuild
that which the enemy tried to destroy.*

Questions for Reflection:
1. What disaster from your past do you need to believe that God can send people to help you recover from?
2. What can you do to prevent yourself from becoming someone who is satisfied with only consuming religious goods and services from the church you attend?
3. For church planters, church-planting team members, ministry leaders, and volunteers: How can you show a greater amount of gratitude and appreciation for the laborers God has sent you?

YEAR THREE
(2015–2016)

Chapter 12

AJ

And when he comes, he will convict the world concerning sin and righteousness and judgment.

—John 16:8

We experienced many miracles in the first two years of our ministry, but God really outdid himself in year three. If year two could be summed up with the words *disaster* and *recovery*, year three could be summed up with the words *miraculous rebuilding.*

By December 2015, the staff of five that I started out with in fall 2013 was down to one—me.

To say I was discouraged would be an understatement.

Even though we had a fair number of volunteer leaders overseeing our various ministries, there was no doubt that in light of my many inadequacies, I needed at least a few full-time people dedicated to pushing the mission of the church forward.

Enter God.

In January 2016, God freed up the financial resources for Bekah, one of the seminarians, to join me as a full-time staff member and help with our internal operations. Adding her was integral to the health of our church because her administrative support freed me up to focus on the things I could do well.

Then, in March, a young professional named AJ also joined the staff full-time to oversee external operations. But because of our financial constraints, we could not pay him a full-time salary.

How exactly, then, could he work full-time?

Only God.

A Modern-Day Prodigal Son

For you to fully appreciate how AJ was able to join our staff full-time without earning a salary, you first need to understand his journey of faith.

AJ grew up in a Christian home and gave his life to the Lord as a teenager. When college began, he joined the military and eventually neglected his faith in Christ. This negligence led to a period of more than 10 years when his life was characterized by sexual immorality, drunkenness, and no accountability to anyone but himself. He did what he wanted whenever he wanted. He traveled wherever he wanted whenever he wanted.

He lived his life on his terms.

He eventually left the military and got a job in the Bay Area as a project manager for a developer and manufacturer of products for the life science research and clinical diagnostics markets. In other words, he was super smart and super talented.

He lived in a condo in the Jack London Square neighborhood of Oakland (the same neighborhood where initially we were going to start the church).

In 2014, he heard about our church through a mailer (another plug for mailers) and began attending our services on and off in the spring of that year. In 2015, God began radically moving in AJ's life. AJ began attending church regularly and joined a small group. He started to serve. He also moved out of the apartment he was living in with his girlfriend without anyone but the Lord leading him to do so.

And then, in the summer of 2015, AJ rededicated his life to Christ and went public with his faith in Jesus through baptism.

A Modern-Day Rich Young Ruler

AJ's radical transformation didn't stop at baptism. By the end of 2015, he began sensing a call into vocational ministry, and he wanted to live out that call by working full-time at THEMOVEMENT.CHURCH.

Because he was making a six-figure salary at his current job and because there was no way we could pay him half of that anytime soon, I told him that joining our ministry was something he really had to pray about. It couldn't be impulsive, it couldn't be boredom with his current job, and it couldn't be foolishness disguised as faith. It had to be God.

After fasting and praying for several days in March 2016, AJ decided to join our staff full-time. How exactly was he able to make it work? He did exactly what the rich, young ruler in Mark 10:17–27 was unable to do: he sold his gold and silver (he literally had gold and silver coins).

As an act of faith and obedience that still gives me the chills today, AJ used a large portion of his life's savings to fund the first six months of his employment.

And for those six months when he wasn't receiving a salary from the church, AJ worked as if he were getting paid the six-figure salary that his previous job had given him.

He led our setup and teardown team and our media team. He facilitated our relationship with Mills College and began improving our internal systems and processes—and so much more.

All on his dime.

Only God could've convicted AJ to leave his life of selfishness and sin and return to him. Only God could've convicted AJ to leave his high-paying job to pursue vocational ministry. Only God could've convicted AJ to put his financial future in jeopardy by selling his gold and silver to fund the first six months of his employment at a church.

Only God can convict people to make irrational changes to their lives that boldly proclaim that Jesus is Lord.

Only God.

Attribute of God #12 – God Is a Convictor

Only God can convict someone to choose him over the pleasures and comforts of the world.

Questions for Reflection:

1. What changes is God convicting you to make?
2. What are the potential consequences of not obeying the convictions God is giving you?
3. For church planters, church-planting team members, ministry leaders, and volunteers: How can you place more trust in God's ability to convict than in your ability to convince the people you are ministering to?

Chapter 13

KDIA 1640

Jabez called upon the God of Israel, saying, "Oh that you would bless me and enlarge my border." . . . And God granted what he asked.

—1 Chron. 4:10

It may not make the most sense why this particular story is being told at this point in the book, but in a few chapters, you'll understand why it needs to be written.

In the beginning of 2016, in addition to welcoming two full-time staff members to the team, we came across a unique opportunity. Out of the blue, I received a phone call from a Bay Area Christian AM radio station.

Someway, somehow, they had found my preaching online and were reaching out to see whether I wanted my Sunday sermons broadcast on their station. When I found out the radio station featured Bible teachers such as Ravi Zacharias, Greg Laurie, and Joyce Meyer, I counted their inquiry a high honor.

They wanted to give me the 8:30 a.m. slot, a prime time for people who listen to the radio on their way to work. Although this wasn't an expense our church had previously budgeted for, I discussed it with the elders, and they believed it was something we should try for six months.

Our motivation wasn't to expand my teaching ministry as much as it was to reach the unchurched and dechurched people in the Bay Area who didn't have a church home. We prayed that as people heard my preaching, they would have the conviction they needed to be part of a church community and, eventually, be drawn to our church.

Only God could've opened the doors for a church that was less than three years old to have their preaching broadcast on the radio. Only God could've given us the favor to be given such a great time slot. Only God could've answered my prayer in the most unexpected of ways for my preaching to be heard by more people.

Only God can expand your influence to spheres beyond your current reach.

Only God.

Attribute of God #13 – God Is a Border-Enlarger

Only God can extend your impact
in ways you never expected.

Questions for Reflection:

1. How has God extended your influence and impact in ways you never expected?

2. How would you want God to extend your influence and impact in the lives of others?

3. For church planters, church-planting team members, ministry leaders, and volunteers: What unplanned but calculated risk may you need to consider in order to enlarge your ministry reach?

Chapter 14

Brook

Now I, Nebuchadnezzar, praise and extol and honor the King of heaven, for all his works are right and his ways are just; and those who walk in pride he is able to humble.

—Dan. 4:37

Now, back to the miraculous rebuilding of our church staff. Remember Brook, one of the seminarians from Chapter 11? Well, on December 20, 2015, she posted this comment on a picture I posted on Facebook, a picture of a Christmas gathering we hosted at our home with our pastoral team and volunteer leaders:

"I felt so completely inadequate, but so grateful that God has put me here. It is truly a pleasure and honor beyond words to serve with such a great team. I would seriously clean toilets if it meant I got to serve with you all and at such a great church with awesome people."

After reading this comment, I believed her. I believed that she really would clean toilets to serve on our team. I thought, "It's this type of person with this type of attitude that I want on our staff." The less entitled you feel *to* ministry, the more effective you are *in* ministry.

But I also knew that if we couldn't pay AJ, there was no way we could pay Brook—unless she had gold and silver coins she was willing to sell.

Once again, the circumstances were perfect for another miracle of God to occur.

A Missionary to Oakland?

During a dinner with my wife and me at a Thai restaurant in Oakland Hills, Brook expressed her interest in joining the church staff. Because of her commitment and work ethic (she worked a full-time job that required at least three hours of total commute time, yet she still put more than 10 hours into the ministry each week), I told her that I would love to have her on the staff, but financially we couldn't make it work. Even if the finances were available, we'd have to start paying AJ first. Unless the church's giving grew exponentially, the soonest I could offer her a paying position was in 18 months.

She was undeterred.

Like many missionaries who leave one country to minister in another, she said she was willing to fund-raise her entire salary.

Without any promises of a full-time salary or any assurances that she could fund-raise enough funds to match what she was making at her safe, secure, great-paying job (she worked in an office that supported churches in the Silicon Valley), she joined our staff full-time as our Outreach and Discipleship Process Coordinator in June 2016.

Only God could've humbled Brook enough to claim that she would be willing to clean toilets if that meant she could be on the team. Only God could've humbled Brook enough to commit herself to asking people for help and fund-raising her salary. Only God could've humbled Brook enough to take a job where she wasn't guaranteed a paycheck until a year and a half later.

Only God can humble someone enough to accept that serving him vocationally is a call to be obeyed and not a right to feel entitled to.

Only God.

Attribute of God #14 – God Is a Humbler
*Only God can replace a spirit of entitlement
with a posture of humility.*

Questions for Reflection:
1. How may God be currently trying to humble you?
2. What are the potential consequences of unchecked pride, arrogance, and entitlement?
3. For church planters, church-planting team members, ministry leaders, and volunteers: What parts or perks of ministry have you become entitled to? What are you going to do to further develop the posture of humility necessary for ministering effectively?

Chapter 15

Our Secret Sauce

Go therefore and make disciples of all nations, baptizing them in the name of the Father and of the Son and of the Holy Spirit, teaching them to observe all that I have commanded you. And behold, I am with you always, to the end of the age.

—Matt. 28:19–20

I want to take one more quick pause from telling you how God miraculously rebuilt our staff team to tell you how emphasizing the importance of 1–1 discipleship relationships became "our secret sauce."

Social media comes with its perils, but I will forever be grateful for and continue to engage with it because, in late 2015, I came across a video posted on Periscope by Mac Lake (a pastor and church leadership development expert) that forever changed how we make disciples at our church.

The video couldn't have been any more than 10 minutes long, but the five questions he asked in it haunted me and our team in the weeks and months to follow. These were the questions:

1. Are those you are discipling making disciples?
2. Have you defined what a disciple looks like?

3. How many disciple-makers do you have in your church?
4. Do you have an easily reproducible system for making disciples?
5. Are you equipping people to be disciple-makers?

The questions haunted me because my answers to questions 1, 2, 4, and 5 were no, and my answer to question 3 was, embarrassingly, less than five.

Because Christ's Great Commission is to go and make disciples, these numbers were unacceptable. The church I had initially envisioned deliberately developed disciples, yet we weren't doing it at all. Something had to change.

The Main Thing

In light of these questions and our embarrassing, unacceptable answers to them, we put together a team of people to create the discipleship development process for our church.

For the first four months of 2016, we met, discussed, and brainstormed. It was a grueling process, but by April, I was prepared to preach a two-part series titled "The Main Thing." I explained why discipleship should be the church's priority. Then I unveiled the first version of our easily reproducible system for making disciples.

Today, as a result of the work we did back then (and our continued emphasis on it since), our answers to questions 1, 2, 4, and 5 are an emphatic yes, and our answer to question 3 is more than 40. We currently have more than 100 people in discipleship relationships, and at least a dozen of them are disciples who are making disciples who are making disciples.

Only God could've directed me, among the millions of videos on the Internet, to that Periscope by Mac Lake. Only God could've surrounded me with just the right team to develop our process for disciple-making. Only God could've placed the conviction on so many people in our church to take disciple-making seriously.

Only God can make disciple-making the main priority of a local church when there are so many lesser priorities to be distracted by.

Only God.

Attribute of God #15 – God Is a Commission-Giver

*Only God can command that the local church
repent of its misprioritization and return to
his original mandate to go and make disciples.*

Questions for Reflection:

1. If you are a follower of Jesus Christ, are you currently discipling someone? If not, why not? If so, are you preparing the person you are discipling to disciple someone else?

2. What are the potential consequences of being a Christian who never disciples someone?

3. For church planters, church-planting team members, ministry leaders, and volunteers: What "good" things in ministry are you doing that could be getting in the way of the best thing in ministry you should be doing—disciple-making?

(See Appendices 3 and 4 for an outline of our discipleship process and the tools we use in our 1–1 Discipleship Relationships.)

Chapter 16

The Stites

And the LORD restored the fortunes of Job, when he had prayed for his friends. And the LORD gave Job twice as much as he had before.

—Job 42:10

Now back to the miraculous rebuilding of the staff team. This particular miracle begins with coffee.

Our church was looking for a vendor to provide coffee for Sunday services. I can't remember exactly how I stumbled upon Slojoy, but when I did, I was immediately interested.

Slojoy was a coffee company started by a husband and wife—Christopher and Brittany Stites—who wanted to use the profits from their company to help fund their church plant in the city of Oakland. How could we not support them?

After purchasing coffee from them for several months, we asked if they would be willing to do pour-overs prior to one of our Sunday services. We were concluding a very special teaching series—"The Main Thing"—and we wanted to provide an extra incentive for people to show up.

They agreed, and Christopher asked if they could also meet with our team afterward to get a little advice about church planting in Oakland.

I couldn't wait.

Church Planting Isn't Easy

In our meeting together following the service, I learned that Christopher, Brittany, and their team were having a difficult time getting their church off the ground. They had been in Oakland for about a year, but they were having a hard time gaining momentum, and their core team members were having a difficult time finding affordable housing. Two people who had moved to Oakland to help them plant their church were planning to return to the city they moved from within the month.

Christopher and Brittany felt defeated and exhausted. They had been going nonstop for a year. Brittany had just had their second child. Christopher was driving for Uber in addition to getting his coffee company and church off the ground.

Because I had traveled down the same entrepreneurial, church-plant road, I felt very empathetic toward their situation. With audacious faith, I suggested that they pray about taking a break from planting their church and attend our church for a while to rest and heal.

Little did I know that simple invitation would end up being the beginning of something very special.

From Resting to Staying

Initially, the plan was for Christopher and Brittany to take three to six months to receive from and form relationships within our church community. Then, when the time was right, we intended to send Christopher and Brittany out with several members of our church to plant their church in the city of Oakland, this time with a little bit more local support. (We wanted to be for Christopher and Brittany what Crossroads Church was for us.)

But just a few weeks into that plan, Christopher and I went for breakfast at the famous Brown Sugar Kitchen in West Oakland.

In a meeting that I will never forget (over the most delicious chicken and waffles in the country), he asked what I thought about his ditching the plans to plant his church—at least for now—to join our team.

I couldn't believe what I was hearing.

Christopher was a Bible college graduate. He had successfully pastored and grown a youth ministry to more than 100 middle school and high school students. He was a phenomenal preacher. He had a passion for leading missional community groups, and in addition to all his skills as a pastor, he was an incredible graphic design artist.

He was the ultimate free agent acquisition, not to mention his wife, Brittany, who was a pastor's daughter and phenomenal leader in her own right.

After their four months of rest and recovery and at our three-year anniversary celebration that September, I had the privilege of praying over Christopher and Brittany after introducing him as our small-group pastor, part-time staff member, and the newest member of our pastoral team. He also agreed to do this unpaid. Are you kidding me?

Only God could've brought Slojoy Coffee to my attention. Only God could've prompted Christopher to ask for help. Only God could've given me the courage to challenge Christopher to rest. Only God could've humbled Christopher enough to lay down his position as a lead pastor and his dream of planting a church to join our team. Only God could've bonded our hearts so quickly. Only God could've known he was exactly the type of leader our church needed to take our ministry in Oakland to the next level.

Remember the disaster we experienced in May 2015? Remember that by the end of 2015, I was the only full-time staff member at the church? By the miraculous hand of God, in September of 2016 (just eight months later), there were four full-time staff members and one part-time staff member. (Only two of them were actually getting paid by the church.) And if that wasn't miraculous enough, the level of leadership competency and ministry experience that this team had was far greater than any other team I had served with in the past. (No shade. Just facts.)

Only God can restore to you exponentially what the enemy stole from you temporarily.

Only God.

Attribute of God #16 – God Is a Restorer

Only God can use a downturn to be
the setup for an upgrade.

Questions for Reflection:

1. How can you give yourself an extended time of rest so God can restore you?

2. What are the potential consequences of not giving yourself this rest?

3. For church planters, church-planting team members, ministry leaders, and volunteers: What are the areas of your life and ministry that you need to persevere in, believing that God can restore?

(See Appendix 5 to read a vision description called "The Leadership Team I See." This was written for our new staff and leadership team in an effort to avoid some of the issues I faced with my first staff and leadership team.)

Chapter 17

Haig

I am making a way in the wilderness and streams in the wasteland.

—Isa. 43:19 NIV

Very quickly, before we go on to the miracles of year four, I have to tell you about one more amazing miracle that took place in year three.

Remember KDIA 1640? In one sense, it was a total failure. After more than six months of programming and 120 broadcasts, we only had three known guests actually attend our church as a result of listening to our radio program. (What a flop!)

But in another sense, it was an absolute success. One of those guests was Haig. He had grown up in a Christian home but hadn't been a member of a church community for more than 15 years. He listened to KDIA on his commute to work. After Haig had listened to our program for several weeks, God convicted him of his need for a Christian community. Haig's very first service was our three-year anniversary service—the one where we introduced Christopher and Brittany. He loved it.

But that's not all.

Early on in our fourth year of ministry, the drummer who had played for us since the church started left the church. We had no idea how we were going to replace him. Come to find out, Haig was a drummer. He's been playing for us ever since. Haig needed a church; we needed a drummer. A "failed" radio program was God's way of solving both of our problems.

Only God.

Attribute of God #17 – God Is a Way-Maker

Only God can leverage our failures as
the way to accomplish his purposes.

Questions for Reflection:

1. What past "failure" has God used to accomplish one of his purposes for your life?

2. What current "failure" may God be preparing to use to accomplish one of his purposes for your life?

3. For church planters, church-planting team members, ministry leaders, and volunteers: How may God desire to use a current ministry "failure" to be the way forward toward your next ministry success?

YEAR FOUR
(2016-2017)

Chapter 18

The Ebuens

Revive me according to Your lovingkindness.

—Ps. 119:88 NASB

To say we were going into our fourth year of ministry with momentum would've been an understatement. Our Sunday attendance had grown 15 percent from the previous year. We had more people in 1–1 discipleship relationships than ever before. People were engaging in midweek community groups at an all-time high. A large percentage of our attendees on Sunday were volunteering to serve on teams. We had baptized 10 new believers and volunteered more than 1,000 hours of community service in Oakland. Our internal giving increased over the previous year by $15,000. We gave more than $20,000 to missions.

Once again, THEMOVEMENT.CHURCH was on the move.

And the miracles kept coming—this time, from farther away than any of us would have ever anticipated.

Green Valley

In the summer of 2016, I was invited to speak at a summer camp for middle school and high school students.

After the camp was over, I met one of the campers, Michaela, who hadn't wanted to be there but needed to so she could chaperone her sister who had a torn ACL. Michaela told me she was deeply impacted by the messages.

She had grown up in a Christian household, but during her last couple of years in high school, she was no longer living a life surrendered to Christ.

In the weeks following the camp, she told her parents she wanted to reengage her relationship with Jesus and start going to THEMOVEMENT.CHURCH. Our church was 40 miles from where they lived in Green Valley, California, but her parents were ecstatic about their daughter's renewed interest in her faith.

They were faithfully committed to a church much closer to where they lived and had been for more than 20 years, but they decided to attend our services a couple of times with Michaela to make sure she felt comfortable with both the drive and our church community.

Little did they know that God had something in store for them, too.

It's a Family Affair

After a handful of services and a few positive experiences with God's work in our church community, Mike and Tara (Michaela's parents) considered that God may be calling them to join our church.

After hearing that our church needed mature Christians to come alongside our newer, younger believers to disciple them and help them grow in their faith, they felt a strong pull toward making our church their new church home. Our emphasis on discipleship really resonated with them. They had been committed to discipleship through their involvement in Bible Study Fellowship (an in-depth, comprehensive Bible class), both attending and teaching, and they discipled young married couples as well.

As involved as they were in their current church, they couldn't shake the fact that God might be up to something *new* in their lives.

After seeking the Lord in prayer, they talked with their pastor to receive his blessing on their transition, and they finished their commitments at their church. (They are a great example of what it looks like to leave a church well.)

With their prior commitments completed, Mike, Tara, and their four daughters took a step of faith and made THEMOVEMENT.CHURCH home.

Only God could've used a camp that Michaela was reluctant to attend to revive her relationship with him. Only God could've convicted Mike and Tara to leave a church they had been committed to for more than 20 years to start attending a church that was more than 40 miles away. Only God could've used Michaela's renewed faith to reinvigorate Mike's and Tara's passion for the local church.

Only God can revive and reinvigorate the faith of those who have been walking with him and serving him for decades.

Only God.

Attribute of God #18 – God Is a Reviver

*Only God can break through the routine of
faith to bring revival to your faith.*

Questions for Reflection:

1. How might the routine of your walk with Christ and the routine of your involvement in the local church be hindering the revival that God wants to bring to your faith?

2. What are the potential consequences of not having your faith revived and renewed?

3. For church planters, church-planting team members, ministry leaders, and volunteers: What are you doing to not let the routines of ministry work be an obstacle to the ongoing revival that God wants you to experience in him?

Chapter 19

Disaster Again?

As for you, you meant evil against me, but God meant it for good, to bring it about that many people should be kept alive, as they are today.

—Gen. 50:20

As 2016 turned to 2017, we led our church through 21 days of corporate prayer and fasting. I had personally practiced the discipline of fasting and prayer and had led our Core Team and church leaders to do it in the past, but this was the first time there was a coordinated effort to get our entire church involved.

To my dismay, before this fast would become a catalyst for more miracles within our church, it almost destroyed the miraculous rebuilding of the prior months.

Hangry

The entire church was encouraged to participate in a 21-day fast, but our staff decided to fast for 40 days.

Some of us were doing liquid-only fasts, some of us a Daniel fast, and others a combination of the two. For all the staff members except me, this was the first time they had attempted an extended fast from certain foods.

The hunger pains, frustration, discomfort—they all hit pretty hard. Toward the end of 40 days, I learned that all the staff members and a few other church leaders were disgruntled with my leadership. Unfortunately, they weren't just keeping these issues to themselves. They were bringing members of the church into these conversations as well—new attendees at that!

In an effort to get to the bottom of it, I called our staff together to listen to their concerns. (I also asked Pastor Christopher to attend this meeting so he could witness and discern what was taking place.) With no hesitation, they rattled off a list of more than 20 ways I had offended them over the last month.

I was hurt, confused, and angry. It felt like déjà vu. Was the same thing that had occurred not even two years ago about to happen again? Was I really this incompetent of a leader? Was I not cut out for this? How much of it was me? How much of it was them? How much of it was a result of the fact that we were all "hangry" and just needed to eat again? How much of it was spiritual warfare?

Thankfully, the truth soon became clear.

Was I Unloving?

I asked Pastor Christopher to help me unpack everything he had witnessed. Because he was serving on staff as well, I told him to be honest about whether the offenses were sin issues, unmet expectations, or some combination of the two. Was he seeing what the rest of the staff members were seeing?

Because I was being perceived as an unloving pastor to both the staff and other members of the church, I also talked to two other members of our pastoral team to help me discern the truth. Was I unloving?

I'm so thankful for their wisdom, counsel, and encouragement during this time. Not only did they ask me the tough questions necessary to discern the truth, but they also talked with the people who had problems with me so they could understand the situation more clearly.

After much counsel, many prayers, and a few sleepless nights, God revealed the problem to me.

Only God.

It was similar to the first disaster, and I refused to let it harm the church again. I was determined to defend the unity of our team.

Reordering Roles

I called another meeting with all the staff members and invited two members of the pastoral team to witness the meeting so they could hold us accountable to reconciliation.

I owned and repented of the ways I had sinned against my staff (failing to keep my word and being inconsistent with one-on-one meetings were my primary sins). But I also made clear the ways in which the staff had sinned against me. That wasn't easy because I didn't want to lose them as I had lost previous staff members. But this was a huge moment in my leadership development, and I couldn't abdicate the position of leadership that God had given me.

I confronted them about ingratitude, gossip, and entitlement. I made it clear that I was not primarily their friend, and, as harsh as it sounded, for our relationships to be healthy, my roles in their life had to be clear. First, I was their boss. Then, I was their pastor. Finally, I was their friend. It cannot be understated how much confusion and pain there can be in a relationship between a pastor and his staff when these three roles are out of order.

By the end of the meeting, we set new expectations, prayed together, and determined to get ourselves back on track.

Stronger Than Ever Before

In the days that followed that meeting, I had individual conversations with each of the staff members in which we experienced true repentance and humility. The peace we experienced *with* one another and the love we had *for* one another, in spite of our sin *against* one another, was something only the Holy Spirit of God could've produced.

What started as another disaster became the very thing I needed to grow into the leader and the pastor God was calling me to be. And it was the exact thing our team needed to strengthen our love for and commitment to one another.

Only God could've positioned Pastor Christopher at just the right place and at just the right time to help us avoid blame and see the truth. Only God could've given me the wisdom to see the true problem. Only God could've given me the courage not to cower.

Only God could've given the staff the patience to forgive my faults and the humility to repent of theirs. Only God could've guarded our unity. Only God could've strengthened our bond.

Only God can take what the enemy intends for evil and turn it into something for our good and his glory.

Only God.

Attribute of God #19 – God Is a Reconciler
*Only God can require repentance within
a team to reconcile relationships on a team.*

Questions for Reflection:
1. In what relationships do you need to repent of sin and ask for forgiveness so reconciliation can take place?
2. What are the potential consequences of not practicing repentance in your relationships?
3. For church planters, church-planting team members, ministry leaders, and volunteers: Are there any unreconciled relationships on your team? If not, praise God! If so, what are you going to do about it?

Chapter 20

Alicia

Our Father in heaven.

—Matt. 6:9

At some point near the beginning of the fast, I received an email from The Learning Channel (TLC). They were taping a show called *My Giant Life,* and they asked if our church would be interested in hosting a singles mixer for a woman starring in their upcoming season. They had visited our website and sensed that our church had the right vibe for their show's goals.

For context, *My Giant Life* showcases the lives of women who are 6′ 6″ or taller, highlighting the many challenges and unique circumstances that being tall brings. The storyline of the woman attending the mixer was a single, Christian virgin who was reentering the dating scene after a bit of a hiatus.

It was one of the most unexpected opportunities I had ever entertained as a pastor, and I was definitely intrigued. My only concern was that I didn't want our church filmed doing something we wouldn't naturally do. Our team was a bit hesitant to move forward with the opportunity. But because I had intended to get our singles together and talk about ways our church could serve them and cater to their unique needs more effectively, we agreed that the idea of hosting a singles mixer wasn't too far of a stretch.

So we moved forward.

In addition to connecting our singles in a unique way, I also sensed that God had something in store for the woman starring on the show. But what God *did* have in store was far beyond anything I could have envisioned.

The Night of the Taping

I was excited. Our singles were excited. Even some of our married couples showed up just to be part of the excitement. Our "little church that could" was going to be on cable television.

We held the event at a nice venue in Berkeley. We all signed waivers (to this day I don't even know what I was signing off on), and then the cameras started to roll.

Alicia walked in and introduced herself to a few of our church members. I facilitated an icebreaker and then transitioned to a conversation about singleness. One of the questions I asked was this: "What are some of the unique challenges you face being single and Christian?"

Alicia bravely shared the difficulty she faced saving herself for marriage. A few of our church members empathized with her and shared similar sentiments.

And then, a few moments later, Alicia unexpectedly walked out of the room.

The cameras followed her.

I had no idea what to do.

When I remembered that we weren't holding this event for the cameras (duh!), I continued leading the conversation even though Alicia and the cameras were no longer in the room.

Alicia eventually returned, and we ended the night with one more icebreaker. A few of our church members were interviewed on camera, and the taping ended. As the camera crew prepared to leave, I sat down with Alicia, and she explained why she left the room so suddenly.

An Unexpected Connection

She said she was overcome by emotion. It turned out that she had no idea this event would be a singles mixer full of church people. She couldn't remember the last time she was among a group of people who believed what she believed, were committed to what she was committed to, and understood the challenges of living a life honoring to God. She had to leave the room because she was crying tears of joy. For the first time in a long time, she felt seen.

Only God.

She also said that she had been looking for a new church community to be a part of. The week before, she had come across our church's website, and when she walked in, she thought she recognized me. What are the chances that the same church she had stumbled upon online would be the same church the TV show she was on would use for the mixer?

Only God.

She ended our conversation by saying, "I don't know how God is going to end up using this show, but I'm definitely going to visit your church."

And just one week later, she did.

All In

Alicia enjoyed her first service so much that even though we were one week into the fast, she joined our corporate fast. She attended our Sunday services and prayer meetings, and she even joined a small group. Within weeks of meeting us at the mixer, she was convinced that this was the community of faith she had been looking for.

But it didn't stop there.

For the last two years, Alicia has grown by leaps and bounds. She has fully surrendered her life to Christ, fully engaged in our church community, and fully committed herself to our mission to overwhelm Oakland with love.

She serves. She gives. She invites. She's even hosted a small group in her home.

Her relationship with Jesus is now characterized by a joy and an enthusiasm that she had previously never experienced. Additionally, some of her closest, most authentic relationships with others are with friends she has in the church.

Only God could've orchestrated this connection. Only God could've compelled us to take advantage of such an unexpected opportunity. Only God could've used a television show to help a woman, who was looking for a man, find a church family.

Only God can use our wants to lead us to our needs.

Only God.

Attribute of God #20 – God Is a Father

Only God can discern between the wants and needs of his children and decide when we should be given either.

Questions for Reflection:

1. What are your wants you may be confusing with your needs?
2. In what areas of your life do you need to place a greater faith in your heavenly Father's desire and ability to provide for your needs?
3. For church planters, church-planting team members, ministry leaders, and volunteers: What are the ministry wants you may be confusing as ministry needs? How can you prevent yourself from falling into the trap of confusing the two?

Chapter 21

Prayer

Hallowed be your name.

—Matt. 6:9

As you can see, a lot happened during our corporate fast in 2017. Fortunately, God wasn't done using this fast to impact our church in meaningful ways. The next miracle was an absolute game-changer. After this miracle took place, our church was never the same again.

During the fast, we met weekly on Monday nights for corporate prayer. Before that, we had corporate prayer meetings once a month, at most. But after the last prayer meeting during the fast, God led me to keep the weekly prayer gatherings going on every Monday night.

Thankfully, I obeyed.

Two years later, we're still meeting every Monday night to pray. We gather to praise God because he is worthy and to petition God because we're needy. At our prayer meetings, our desperation and God's divinity collide. We've discovered along the way that prayer isn't primarily about asking for God's blessing *on* the ministry; prayer is the work *of* the ministry.

We've experienced answered prayers, the power and presence of God in palpable ways, and an increased awe and wonder of our holy God. We are convinced that God hears our prayers and is pleased by our seeking him.

But as good as all of that sounds, a weekly prayer meeting wasn't all God had in store for us when it came to corporate prayer.

There was so much more.

A Corporate Prayer Culture

As our weekly prayer meetings gained momentum, God burdened my heart to make corporate prayer an even greater priority. I had read about the corporate prayer meetings at the Brooklyn Tabernacle in *Fresh Wind, Fresh Fire* by Jim Cymbala, so I googled the author and the term *corporate prayer*.

The second search result was "Transcript for Advancing a Culture of Prayer in Your Church," a talk by Pastor Daniel Henderson at a conference in 2012. Until then, I had never heard of Daniel Henderson, but the contents of his talk resonated with me very deeply. I wanted our church to have the type of prayer culture he was describing. The following three excerpts from his talk were exactly what I needed to give me the conviction I needed to lead our church in the direction God had for us:

1. There's a difference between a prayer program and a prayer culture.
2. There's a difference between a church that prays and a praying church.
3. The only enduring motive for prayer is that God is worthy to be sought. That never changes—never changes. If you want to see a culture of prayer, you've just got to be captivated with that. God's worthy.[1]

As a result of these convictions, it became more important to me to develop a corporate prayer *culture*, not just having a corporate prayer meeting. And by God's grace, it happened.

We developed 10 corporate prayers that we consistently prayed. We started praying together in our Sunday gatherings,

---

1. Daniel Henderson, "Advancing a Culture of Prayer in Your Church," September 21, 2012, *Revive Our Hearts*, https://www.reviveourhearts.com/events/true-woman-12/advancing-culture-prayer-your-church/transcript/.

midweek groups, and all our volunteer team meetings. Our staff began meeting weekly to pray, separate from our weekly staff meeting, and our pastoral team began meeting biweekly to pray together, separate from our monthly pastoral team meetings.

What's important to understand is that we didn't start praying together in all these ways for the sake of being able to say we prayed together. We started praying together in all these ways because God graciously revealed to us that he is *worthy* of us doing so.

As the one, true, and holy God, he is *worthy* of our prayers of praise and adoration. As the all-powerful, all-knowing, and all-loving God, he is *worthy* of our prayers of petition and supplication. As the gracious, merciful, and supremely compassionate God, he is *worthy* of our prayers of repentance and confession. And most of all, because of his holiness, he is also worthy of the time, effort, energy, and humility that is required to pray these prayers *together*.

The miracle that God did in our church was not that we became a church that prays together. The miracle God performed was that he transformed us into a church that prays together primarily for the purpose of *worshipping* him.

Only God could've led us to see that we shouldn't pray merely because we need something from God; we pray primarily because we were designed to give worship to God. Only God could've convicted us to believe that his worthiness is more beautiful than his usefulness. Only God could've revealed to us that until who he *is* becomes our motivation for seeking him, what he can do will never fully and finally satisfy.

Becoming a worshipping church was God's goal. Developing a culture of corporate prayer was God's way.

Only God.

Attribute of God #21 – God is Holy

Only God can reveal that the ultimate purpose of praying to God is worshipping God.

Questions for Reflection:

1. Why do you or don't you pray?
2. How could worship as the primary motive for your prayers transform your prayer life?
3. For church planters, church-planting team members, ministry leaders, and volunteers: What are you doing to develop a culture of corporate prayer at your church? What are the potential consequences of not doing anything?

(See Appendices 6 and 7 for a list of our 10 corporate prayers and a vision description of the corporate prayer culture we've committed ourselves to creating.)

Chapter 22

Elmhurst Community Prep

The heart of man plans his way, but the LORD establishes his steps.

—Prov. 16:9

One of our primary prayer requests during our corporate fast was that God would open up the doors to a new meeting space for our Sunday services. Lisser Hall, the auditorium at Mills College where we had been meeting for three and a half years, needed to be renovated. Because there were no other venues on campus that would work for us, it was time for us to move.

God would have to come through again.

And true to form, yet another miracle awaited.

Kilian

As we searched for a new location, we asked one of Oakland's city council members to advise us. She recommended that if we really wanted to have a positive impact on the city, we needed to partner with the public schools. She explained that the health of the public school was integral to the health of a neighborhood.

We were sold.

She connected us with a few principals who might be interested in a partnership, and we were well on our way. After a few of her connections didn't work out, I overheard that a church in our denomination, which had previously been meeting at Elmhurst Community Prep (a public middle school in East Oakland), was closing down. We immediately scheduled a meeting with Kilian Betlach, the principal of Elmhurst, to see if he would be interested in allowing us to rent the space.

Without much hesitation at all, he agreed.

Although Kilian was not a believer in Jesus, the pastor who had previously led the church that met there had left such a positive impression on Kilian that he even asked the pastor to officiate his wedding.

Only God.

Relocated Meeting Space, Redefined Mission Field

As grateful as I was for a new place to meet, I sensed that God was doing much more than opening the doors for a new venue for our services.

Discontent had been surfacing within me about our approach to overwhelming Oakland with love. Until that point, we volunteered hundreds of hours of community service—cleaning the streets, working at the food bank, and hosting racial reconciliation conversations. We even donated time and financial resources to a couple of Oakland public schools.

But as great and well received as those things were, I felt as if we were spread thin and merely placing Band-Aids on issues that would continue to cause problems for our city. We weren't serving in a way that would lead to long-lasting, systemic change.

Then God gave me a vision. Instead of our church being a Band-Aid that covered up the wounds of our city, we would become a balm that would focus on *healing* those wounds.

No longer would we agree to every volunteer opportunity that came our way. It was time to trade in an unrealistic desire to serve everyone in Oakland sporadically for a more intentional approach of loving a specific neighborhood in Oakland, over an extended period of time, *consistently*.

Elmhurst Community Prep wouldn't just be our new meeting space; it would become our new mission field. Our approach would be simple. We would focus on three specific, concentric circles of service in the Elmhurst community of East Oakland. First, we would serve the faculty and staff of the school. Second, we would serve the students and their families. Finally, we would serve the neighborhood surrounding the school. We would do this month after month, year after year, until deep, lasting, systemic change both in the school and in the neighborhood was a reality.

I had never had such clarity about our church's mission. But more than just the clarity, I never had so much excitement, either.

Only God could've guided us to a meeting space that would lead us to our mission field. Only God could've guided us to serve our city more effectively by serving a specific neighborhood more intentionally. Only God could've guided us to embrace a strategy for service that we had very little experience executing.

Because only God knows the destination, only God can guide the way.

Only God.

Attribute of God #22 – God Is a Guider

*Only God can direct the steps that getting
to his destination demands.*

Questions for Reflection:

1. How have you submitted yourself to God's guidance in your life?

2. What are the potential consequences of not submitting yourself to God's guidance?

3. For church planters, church-planting team members, ministry leaders, and volunteers: Where is God guiding your ministry to go next? Are you committed to whatever steps he may call you to take to get there?

Chapter 23

EightX

The LORD said to Abram, after Lot had separated from him, "Lift up your eyes and look from the place where you are, northward and southward and eastward and westward, for all the land that you see I will give to you and to your offspring forever."

—Gen. 13:14–15

Even though moving to a new location and emphasizing serving the school we were meeting in was a lot to take on at once, God had more in store.

We had been meeting at Elmhurst for no more than two months when I came across the following words by Tim Keller on Facebook (another shout-out to the positive impact of social media): "The single best way to reach non-Christians is to start new churches. The transitional new community creates space for outsiders to plug in."[2]

In the original vision I had shared in my condo during the Catch the Vision tour, I said that I envisioned a church that methodically multiplied itself. But until that point, we had no strategy for doing so. And that wasn't the only problem.

2. Timothy Keller, *Facebook.com*, May 28, 2017.

In addition to being uneasy about not having a plan for planting another church, I had also become uneasy about our church's growth—or lack thereof.

After almost four years in ministry, we found ourselves unable to grow our Sunday attendance beyond 150 adults and kids. And we had tried everything. Our inability to grow our church more, combined with the words of Tim Keller, caused me to think that maybe our church would grow differently.

Instead of growing one location larger than 150 people, what if God was calling us to send current members to plant another church as our means of growth? What if instead of being one church serving one public school in the city of Oakland, we needed to become two churches serving two public schools?

I asked Pastor Christopher what he thought. Was God still calling him to become a church planter and lead pastor of his own church? He was intimidated by what it would require, and he was simultaneously invigorated by the vision. God was moving.

The staff and the rest of the pastoral team were excited as well. By June, we decided that in the fall of 2020, we were going to plant our first church, and Pastor Christopher would lead it.

Then the vision got even bigger.

God-Size It

While we began making our preliminary plans to plant our first church, I was also reading a book called *God Dreams* by Will Mancini and Warren Bird. It was a book about having a vision that brings focus to your church's future. As it relates to vision, they wrote:

> The idea of "God-sizing it" doesn't mean making it ridiculously large in scope; it means enlarging the faith of your people in your time and place based on your resources. God-honoring vision comes in all shapes and sizes. . . . You must stretch the mind with an absurd idea, bold outcome, or a daring destination, centered in God's pleasure. Remember that your ability to be audacious is connected to God, not to a sense of over-confidence. Does the idea immediately foster a spirit of God dependence?[3]

These words encouraged me to move our vision of planting one church in 2020 beyond what I could see was possible and pursue a dream that couldn't be achieved unless God intervened.

With audacious faith, I drafted a plan to become a family of *eight* churches serving *eight* public schools in the city of Oakland over the next *eight* years.

I called it our EightX Vision.

In 2020, we would send Pastor Christopher to plant church #2. In 2023, we would send Pastor Spencer (one of the original members of our Core Team whom I had met at Crossroads Church) to plant church #3, and Pastor Christopher would send out someone from his church to plant church #4. Then in 2026, each of our four churches

---

3. William Bird and Will Mancini, *God Dreams* (Nashville: B&H Publishing, 2016), 154.

would each plant another church, making us a family of eight churches.

I was excited!

During our four-year anniversary service, we were privileged to have Principal Kilian Betlach join us and speak of all the ways we had positively impacted the school through our community service in the first five months we had been meeting there. After his testimony, I cast the vision to our church that I had a dream of multiplying this type of impact eight times over.

I asked our church if they could imagine becoming a family of churches serving eight principals in the city of Oakland. I asked if they could imagine becoming a church serving eight faculties, eight student bodies, and eight neighborhoods.

Our church received the vision with enthusiasm and excitement. For the first time in four years of existence as a church, we had a crystal clear picture of what overwhelming Oakland with love *actually* looked like. We were pumped!

Only God could've used our failures as a catalyst for thinking differently about our future. Only God could've kept something small so we could think differently about becoming big. Only God could've convinced us that sending people out (church multiplication) was of higher value in the kingdom of God than keeping people in (church preservation).

Only God can transform someone who only dreamed self-serving dreams to become a person committed to dreaming God-sized, God-honoring dreams.

Only God.

Attribute of God #23 – God Is a Dream-Giver

*Only God can inspire you to wholeheartedly
pursue dreams that cannot be accomplished
unless his power is present.*

Questions for Reflection:

1. What is the God-sized, God-honoring dream that you have for your life?
2. What are the potential consequences of not having a God-sized, God-honoring dream?
3. For church planters, church-planting team members, ministry leaders, and volunteers: What is the God-sized, God-honoring dream you have for your church or ministry?

**YEAR FIVE
(2017–2018)**

Chapter 24

#METOO

He heals the brokenhearted and binds up their wounds.

—Ps. 147:3

As our fifth year of ministry got underway, we planned three services in November to encourage people to invite their friends to church. Over the course of the three services, we preached the following messages:

- "The Power of an Invitation: How Your Ask Could Be Their Answer"
- "Sinners Favored: How God Really Feels about Your Filth"
- "#METOO: A Word of Encouragement for Survivors of Sexual Assault"

To prepare for the third message, I asked one of the women in our congregation to recommend some resources for those in our church community who had been impacted by the violent crime of sexual assault. She had already openly shared about her experience as a survivor of sexual assault. She recommended an organization called Bay Area Women Against Rape (BAWAR). She had a positive experience working with them, but she mentioned that because call volume was high, sometimes it was difficult to get an appointment.

How God would overcome this obstacle would prove, yet again, that nothing is impossible for him.

What Were the Chances?

At the conclusion of the "Sinners Favored" message, I let our congregation know about the #METOO message the following week. Then I made myself available to meet first-time guests as I typically do. Alicia (from the TLC show) introduced me to a couple of guests she had invited. One of her guests was Sarai, who asked if she could talk to me for a minute.

Sarai said that she used to be a pastor at a church in Mountain View and that a couple of years before, while pursuing her doctorate in ministry, she wrote her dissertation on sexual violence in the Bible. After hearing about the #METOO message that was going to be preached the next week, she offered to help in any way she could. She said that though she still had an itinerant preaching ministry, her job now was executive director of a non-profit organization called Bay Area Women Against Rape.

Only God.

I couldn't believe it. What were the chances? When I asked her why she had joined us for church that day, she told me it had to be God. That morning as she was scrolling through stories on her Instagram feed, she came across a video message from Alicia inviting people to church (another plug for the potential positive impact of social media). After watching the brief video invitation, she sensed that she was supposed to attend our service.

Only God.

But as much of a miracle as her attending our church service that day was, the even greater miracle was the help she was able to provide in the weeks that followed.

Just the Support I Needed

Sarai ended up supporting our church in two incredible ways. First, she directed me to a few biblical texts that she thought would be helpful for my message the following week. I ended up choosing the account of Amnon and Tamar in 2 Samuel 13.[4]

But even more helpful than her direction for my message was her presence and insight at a gathering we hosted for survivors of sexual assault several days after the #METOO message. Not only did she help me frame the evening, but she also helped me facilitate it. Because of her presence, the women who attended were comfortable and transparent with their stories in a way I don't believe they would've been without her there.

By God's grace, all who attended the meeting that night experienced honesty, authenticity, compassion, empathy, relief, and an incredible sense of hope. Our church didn't need to worry about our calls getting through to BAWAR; we had direct access to their executive director.

Only God could've brought Alicia's Instagram story to Sarai's attention. Only God could've convicted and compelled Sarai to attend the service that Sunday. Only God could've provided me with exactly the person I needed to help me minister best to those impacted by sexual assault.

Only God, through the power of his Holy Spirit and the cleansing blood of Jesus Christ, can bring peace and healing to survivors of sexual assault.

Only God.

---

4. "The Tension: How Has Sexual Assault Become So Common and Pervasive in American Culture?" *THEMOVEMENT.CHURCH*, https://themovement.church/metoo.

Attribute of God #24 – God Is a Healer

Only God can administer healing to our pains
for which there is no earthly cure.

Questions for Reflection:

1. What are the pains you have experienced that the world has no cure for?
2. What would it look like for you to trust and believe in God to heal you of those pains?
3. For church planters, church-planting team members, ministry leaders, and volunteers: How are you creating spaces for those who have experienced traumatic circumstances to be ministered to?

Chapter 25

Ellis and Cindy

God, our God, shall bless us.

—Ps. 67:6

My parents attend the church I pastor, and it is absolutely a miracle of God.

It is a miracle because for much of my childhood (especially my teenage years), I was selfish—fully consumed by me, myself, and I—and didn't help out much around the house. I wasn't the best sibling to my younger brothers and sister, and often, I flat out wasn't present. I rarely acknowledged the sacrifices my parents made that allowed me to grow up in a home most kids would envy. I thought only of my needs, my wants, and my concerns.

What made matters worse is that I knew better.

I was introduced to Jesus Christ at a young age, became a Christian, and was raised to know that Christ-likeness was best displayed by sacrificial service. Unfortunately, how I behaved in the home did not reflect what I knew about Christ.

So how do parents of such a selfish son eventually see that same son as their pastor?

Only God!

Firm Foundation

But the miracle to appreciate isn't only a second chance to live as a more God-honoring son. The greater miracle is the firm foundation God blessed me with through such God-fearing parents. Because of their love for the Lord and for each other, I grew up with a front-row seat to what godly living actually looked like. Forgiveness toward each other, sacrifice for their kids, patience with their parents and siblings, humility before God, love for Jesus, reliance on the Holy Spirit, commitment to the local church, faithfulness to their pastor, investment in others—I saw them model it all.

And when they didn't get it right, they modeled for me what it looked like to handle sin and shortcomings in a godly way. They confessed, apologized, and repented. They showed my siblings and me what it looked like to be honest about sin and shame. They showed us what working out your faith with fear and trembling looks like in real life. I knew the grace of Jesus Christ could be real for *me* because I knew the grace of Jesus Christ was real for *them*.

Much of how they lived and what they modeled for me gives me the strength and stability to be the pastor I am today. Much of the effectiveness of my pastoring can be attributed to the excellence of their parenting. Much of my faith can be traced back to *their* faithfulness.

Only God could've blessed me with the type of parents that would best prepare me to be the person and pastor I am today. Only God could've blessed my parents with the humility to receive pastoral care from their son. Only God could've blessed me with a miracle I never saw coming—partnering with my parents in ministry.

Only God can bless you with exactly the right people to love you.

Only God.

Attribute of God #25 – God Is a Blesser

*Only God can bless you through the people
he chooses to love you.*

Questions for Reflection:

1. Who are the people in your life through whom God has blessed you?
2. How should you show honor and appreciation to the people through whom God has blessed you?
3. For church planters, church-planting team members, ministry leaders, and volunteers: Who are the people God has placed in your life, the ones who have shaped and formed you into the minister you are today? How should you honor and appreciate them?

Chapter 26

$45,000 in 45 Days

Behold, God is my helper; the LORD *is the upholder of my life.*

—Ps. 54:4

In January 2018, our church was on the brink of experiencing financial hardship for the first time since we started.

Most church plants plan to be self-sustaining from tithes and offerings of their own congregation after three to four years. Because of this, many churches that financially support church plants stop doing so between years three and four.

Unfortunately, even though we were more than four years old, we weren't yet self-sustaining. We still relied on support from other churches for about 25 percent of our annual budget. We were behind on the internal giving we had projected, and we hadn't raised enough external support to cover the deficit.

I hesitantly reached out to two of our supporting churches who were not planning to financially support us in 2018. They had already been so generous, and I felt that it looked bad to ask them for more money. But I also knew that if looking bad was my concern, then leadership was no longer for me.

With that in mind, I let the two churches know our financial situation, and I asked them to consider supporting us for one more year. Forty-five days later, our church received two checks totaling $45,000.

Only God could've given me the humility and courage to ask for help. Only God could've given the churches the financial resources to extend their partnership unexpectedly. Only God could've provided our church with so much money in such a short time.

Only God can help you when you probably shouldn't be receiving any more help.

Only God.

Attribute of God #26 – God Is a Helper
Only God can help you beyond the ways
you expect him to uphold you.

Questions for Reflection:
1. How has God recently been your helper?
2. How might you need to humble yourself so God can be a helper to you?
3. For church planters, church-planting team members, ministry leaders, and volunteers: Who do you need to ask for help so your ministry can go to the next level? What are the potential consequences of neglecting to ask for help?

(See Appendix 8 to read a document called "The Financial Stewardship I See." I wrote it to act as a filter for the decisions we make with church finances.)

Chapter 27

13 Pastors!

The whole body, nourished and knit together through its joints and ligaments, grows with a growth that is from God.

—Col. 2:19

In our membership meeting in August 2018, the church affirmed the installation of two pastors and two pastoral apprentices, giving us a total of seven pastors and two pastoral apprentices. Nine pastors? How is that possible?

Only God.

Since our church started, we have always been blessed with an abundance of biblically qualified men who desired to serve the church as pastors, so much so that by the beginning of our second year, I served alongside a team of five pastors and one pastoral apprentice. That is a miracle all by itself. (Very few church plants have the luxury of a pastoral team within its first two years.)

Having this team in place was critical. When the disaster occurred in 2015, if we hadn't had a team of pastors in place to help lead me and the congregation through the relational issues I went through with our executive pastor, I don't think the church would have survived.

Several pastors have come and gone through the years, but by God's grace, he has continued to send men with a pastoral calling on their lives to help shepherd the people of the church. Here were the pastors as of that membership meeting in August 2018:

1. Me
2. Rich Johnstone (faithful from the beginning)
3. Ellis Paz (Yup, my dad became one of the pastors.)
4. Spencer Romero (I'll tell you more about him in the next chapter.)
5. Christopher Stites (the best free agent acquisition ever)
6. AJ DeLaFuente (from mailer to minister! Only God.)
7. Mike Ebuen (His commute didn't get shorter, but his commitment got stronger.)

The pastoral apprentices we put forward were Alex Sung and Mike Terry. (I can't wait to tell their stories one day.)

After that meeting, I had conversations with four additional men who expressed a desire to discern whether God may be calling them into pastoral ministry. What church of 150 people needs 13 pastors?

What I discerned happening was that God was equipping us with the pastoral leadership to support our vision of becoming a family of eight churches in the city of Oakland. God wasn't blessing us with an abundance of pastors so they could all shepherd one church. He was blessing us with an abundance of pastors so not only would we be prepared to send out a lead pastor to each of our future church plants, but we could also send out pastoral *teams* to each of our future church plants.

Only God.

But the sheer number of pastors in our church is not the only miracle. How we function together is miraculous, too.

Unity Amid Diversity

Even though we are diverse in age, ethnicity, educational background, beliefs, and pastoral experience, we have found a way to lead together, preach together, pray together, and shepherd together.

We have checked our agendas at the door and placed our egos at the foot of the cross. And when we've had disagreements (because we often do), we have learned to work it out like godly people should—patiently, humbly, and prayerfully. We have submitted ourselves to the authority of scripture, we have submitted ourselves to one another, we have submitted ourselves to the church, and we have submitted ourselves to shepherd and serve God's church *together*.

If left to ourselves and the desires of our flesh, we wouldn't have chosen one another. Instead, we would have chosen pride, power, and individualism. But God has done a miracle.

Only God could've given us unity in the midst of so much diversity. Only God could've given us humility in the midst of so much ability. Only God could've given us the collective desire to become a team of pastors who leverage their God-given authority not for selfish gain but for selfless and sacrificial service to the bride of Christ.

Only God can take a diverse group of individuals, all from different directions, and bring them together in such a way that they form an unbreakable bond committed to moving toward the same destination.

Only God.

Attribute of God #27 – God Is a Knitter

Only God can knit together the type of team
that the world couldn't keep together.

Questions for Reflection:

1. What can you do to pursue unity with people who are unlike you?
2. What can you do to work better together with people who are unlike you?
3. For church planters, church-planting team members, ministry leaders, and volunteers: How are you creating opportunities for people who may be different than you to join your ministry?

(See Appendices 9 and 10 to read the two documents that help keep our pastoral team unified and on the same page.)

Chapter 28

Spencer

Now may the God of peace himself sanctify you completely, and may your whole spirit and soul and body be kept blameless at the coming of our Lord Jesus Christ. He who calls you is faithful; he will surely do it.

—1 Thess. 5:23–24

As this book comes to an end, the story of our church cannot be fully appreciated without telling the story of God's miraculous work in the life of Spencer Romero.

I met Spencer at Crossroads Church in 2011. He was 19, unsaved, unemployed, and unaware of his need for a Savior. He was raising his two-year-old son, Peyton, with his girlfriend, Lanae. He began attending church because Lanae gave him the ultimatum that if he didn't start going, she would leave him.

After he attended our church for a few months, I had the opportunity to sit with him, hear his story, and share the gospel with him:

For the wages of sin is death, but the free gift of God is eternal life in Christ Jesus our Lord.

—Rom. 6:23

After explaining to him the meaning of this scripture, I asked if he believed this, and without hesitation, he said yes.

Only God.

From that point forward, his testimony has been marked by *yes* after *yes* after *yes*.

In March 2012, he got baptized. Although he was a new believer, he started leading two Bible study groups—one with his college football team and one with his family. He shared the gospel with everyone he knew. When he and Lanae joined the leadership team of our high school ministry, he led a small group of high school students as well.

By mid 2012, he was preaching in the high school ministry. He confessed his unconfessed sins, took difficult steps of obedience (giving up on his dream to play college football and taking seriously his responsibility to provide for his family), and committed with Lanae to join the Core Team of our church plant.

Then he proposed to Lanae, and they got married the week after we held our first preview service in Jack London Square.

Only God.

And this was just the beginning of his miraculous story.

Serving Everywhere

When it came to serving on the Core Team for our church plant, Spencer did almost everything. He served on our guest services team by helping park cars. He served on our setup and teardown team by unloading our U-Haul. And he served on our pastoral team by preaching on Sundays. He led our prayer ministry, a small group, and, most important, his family.

Then, in summer 2015, I had the privilege of ordaining this faithful servant as a pastor.

Only God.

So why did I wait this far into our church's history to tell you his story? Because it was during our fifth year that Spencer experienced his most fruitful year.

Fruitfulness Follows Faithfulness

When the vision was cast to become a family of eight churches, Spencer initially (it's still a few years out) accepted God's call to be a lead pastor of one of the church plants.

Then, in preparation to answer that future call, he accepted God's assignment for him to take over the leadership responsibilities of our student ministry (6th–12th graders). The same young man who was once ministered to by a student ministry was now leading ours.

In January, his team took a dozen kids to a student winter camp. God moved powerfully through Spencer to reach the students, many of them who were new to the church, in a unique way. Then, on Easter Sunday, he and his team baptized eight of the students who had attended the winter camp and had given their lives to the Lord.

In August, he was invited to be a camp speaker for a student summer camp. Once again, God used him powerfully, not just to reach our students who attended but to reach students from another church who were there as well. After the camp, two more students got baptized.

I was so blessed to see Spencer, who had served God so faithfully for several years in the shadows, be given opportunities to use his God-given gifts in more visible ways to connect people to the same gospel that had so powerfully impacted him.

Only God could've saved Spencer so quickly. Only God could've sanctified Spencer so thoroughly. Only God could've gifted Spencer so generously.

Only God can give someone the patience and perseverance required to endure the process.

Only God.

Attribute of God #28 – God Is a Sanctifier

Only God can assign the mundane as a means of making someone into his masterpiece.

Questions for Reflection:

1. How are you stewarding the small, seemingly insignificant tasks God has given you?

2. What are the potential consequences of not stewarding your season in the shadows well?

3. For church planters, church-planting team members, ministry leaders, and volunteers: How will you prevent yourself from growing weary or becoming resentful of the many small, seemingly insignificant, behind-the-scenes responsibilities that ministry requires of you?

Chapter 29

Five-Year Anniversary

*Bless the LORD, O my soul, and forget not all his benefits, who
forgives all your iniquity, who heals all your diseases, who redeems
your life from the pit, who crowns you with steadfast love and
mercy.*

—Ps. 103:2–4

I'd been looking forward to celebrating this day for a
long time. For the church's five-year anniversary, we had
planned to introduce the new branding of our church (which
incorporated our EightX vision) and hear another testimony
from Principal Kilian Betlach about our positive impact on
the school. We planned to hear a testimony from a couple
who'd suffered and overcome infidelity, and also ordain AJ as
a pastor. Then, I was going to preach a message that would
excite and envision our church for the *next* five years.

But God had slightly different plans.

A week before the anniversary service, while in Portland,
Oregon, I got a severe bacterial infection in my right eye. Due
to the excruciating pain, I was rushed to an emergency room
in Portland. The doctors gave me medication to temporarily
ease the pain, but the next morning it was worse.

When I returned to Oakland and saw an ophthalmologist, she placed me on four different drops for my eye and four different oral medications that I needed to take every 30 minutes. She let me know that I was in danger of losing my eyeball and I needed to monitor it very closely. It was bad.

As much as I still wanted to preach in our five-year anniversary service, there was no way I would be able to. The pain was too great. My right eye couldn't even tolerate reading or looking at a computer screen for longer than five minutes. I didn't have the strength to put together a message, let alone preach it.

Thankfully, Spencer, with less than a week's notice, agreed to facilitate the service and preach the message.

Kilian's testimony turned out great, and AJ's ordination (which I still got to be part of) was awesome. Spencer's message was powerful (as usual), but no one could have expected the impact that Wayne and Marcie's testimony would have on our church family when they shared how they overcame infidelity in their marriage.

Wayne and Marcie

Two years earlier, as Marcie and Wayne were approaching their 10-year wedding anniversary, Marcie found out that Wayne had been cheating on her. When this happened, Wayne gave me a call to reach out for help. I rushed to their house to do my best to bring the peace of God to their situation.

Wayne and Marcie's story was devastating. The pain and regret were palpable.

Marcie was angry and broken. Wayne was apologetic and sorrowful. But both of them, despite the circumstances, wanted to do whatever they could to make things work.

Only God.

In the months that followed, Wayne surrendered his life to the Lord and got baptized. They began seeing my parents for marriage counseling. Things seemed to have turned around. Unfortunately, Wayne cheated again.

Marcie was broken—again. Wayne was sorrowful—again. God was gracious—again.

Marcie insisted that Wayne move out of the house for a time. They continued marriage counseling with my parents, and they also saw a professional for individual counseling.

Slowly but surely, they rebuilt trust. Slowly, they reached reconciliation. Forgiveness was eventually extended, and a deep love and commitment for each other were reignited.

Only God.

When Wayne and Marcie shared their testimony, live from the stage during our five-year anniversary service, there wasn't a dry eye in the house.

Their courage and transparency in sharing their story of hurt and healing moved us all. We all were encouraged by God's power and grace to take what was broken and turn it into something beautiful. God's hand in their story was undeniable.

Only God in his infinite goodness and grace could've allowed us the privilege of celebrating such a powerful miracle on such a momentous occasion. Only God could've made our five-year anniversary service 10 times better than I could have ever imagined. Only God could've humbled me by making it evident through my inability to contribute significantly to the service that *he* was the one building his church.

Only God can redeem the effects of a fallen world for the fame of his name.

Only God.

Attribute of God #29 – God Is a Redeemer

Only God can create beauty from ashes.

Questions for Reflection:

1. What are the struggles of your life that God has redeemed to create beauty in your life?
2. What are the struggles of your life that you need to persist in believing that God will create something beautiful from?
3. For church planters, church-planting team members, ministry leaders, and volunteers: How are you providing spaces and opportunities for people in your church to share their stories of redemption? What are the potential consequences of not providing these opportunities?

Chapter 30

Pseudomonas

Come, let us return to the Lord; for he has torn us, that he may heal us; he has struck us down, and he will bind us up.

—Hosea 6:1

To this day, I have absolutely no vision in my right eye. It isn't pitch-black, but it is completely blurred. Believe it or not, I wrote this book with vision only in my left eye.

Only God. (Thank God for two eyes. For real.)

The infection I got in my eye while I was in Portland—known as pseudomonas—came from a bacteria found in air, water, and dirt. How I caught it is unknown, but after three months of an intense amount of antibiotics, the infection is gone, the pain has subsided, and I am no longer in danger of losing my right eyeball.

In late fall 2019, when my right eye is expected to be completely stabilized, I will need a cornea replacement surgery to regain sight. A year after I have the cornea replacement, I will most likely need cataract removal surgery—collateral damage from the bacterial infection.

I decided to close this book with this particular story because the last miracle God did in the first five years of

THEMOVEMENT.CHURCH was a miracle that God did for me.

Did he heal my eye?

No.

It's so much better than that.

Vision > Sight

As cheesy as this may sound, even though my eyesight to see things in this world has been cut in half, I feel as if my vision to see God, his character, and his goodness has doubled.

When I was experiencing unbearable physical pain, I saw the supernatural *comfort* of God. Comfort that eased me. Comfort that empathized with me. Comfort that encouraged me. Now I see God as a comforter more clearly than ever before.

When I was experiencing extreme emotional fatigue, I saw the supernatural *power* of God. Power that sustained me. Power that rested me. Power that strengthened me. Now I can see God as powerful more clearly than ever before.

When I was experiencing extreme spiritual doubt, I saw the supernatural *faithfulness* of God. Faithfulness that reminded me of his character. Faithfulness that showered me with his love. Faithfulness that pointed me to the cross. Now I can see God as faithful more clearly than ever before.

Because I could see God more clearly, my joy could be found in him more completely. I now believe that God's allowing the bacteria to infect my eye was the best thing that could have ever happened to me. That God would love me enough to allow something like this to happen so I could see him more clearly is a great blessing.

But it's not only my view of God that became clearer; I also grew in my ability to empathize with the difficulties of others. I can now "see" and relate to others' pains, doubts, fears, and frustrations like never before. Experiencing unexplainable, unexpected pain helped me be more sensitive to the unexplainable, unexpected pain of others.

Only God could've diminished my sight to multiply my vision. Only God could've disabled me to enable me. Only

God could've slowed me down physically so I could mature spiritually.

Only God could've caused me to pause. Only God could've convicted me to invest the time to reflect on and write about the miracles I've experienced in my life and through our church over the last several years. Only God could've opened my eyes to see what I failed to see for so long.

It has *always* been because of him; it has *never* been because of me.

Only God.

Attribute of God #30 – God Is a Wounder
Only God can wound you to bless you.

Questions for Reflection:
1. What are the physical limitations you have that God might use to draw you closer to him?
2. What blessings might actually come as a result of the physical limitations you may have?
3. For church planters, church-planting team members, ministry leaders, and volunteers: How will you recount the miracles that God has performed in your church and ministry?

Closing Thoughts

To THEMOVEMENT.CHURCH. If your personal miraculous story is not referenced in this book, I apologize. I feel a little bit like John when he wrote at the end of his Gospel, "Now there are also many other things that Jesus did. Were every one of them to be written, I suppose that the world itself could not contain the books that would be written" (John 21:25).

Your story is no less miraculous than the ones I included in this book. There wasn't any way I could write about everybody. Thanks for understanding.

This is a story that God is writing, and we get to be part of it. Let's steward it well. Let's celebrate it often. Let's share it everywhere. God is worthy, and we will be held accountable for what we did with what we were privileged to be part of.

To our extended church family, specifically the members of our partner churches. Thank you for giving to missions. Thank you for believing in church planting. Thank you for giving above and beyond your tithes and offerings to support what God is doing all around the world.

These miraculous stories are a direct result of your faith-filled generosity. Your giving is impacting the eternities of real people in Oakland and beyond. I pray that as you read these stories, you will feel a real sense of joy, knowing that this fruit is a result of seeds *you* have sown. Keep trusting. Keep stretching. Keep giving. More of God's miracles are in store.

To fellow church planters and pastors. Document the stories of God's miraculous hand at work in your church. I wrote this book more for me than I did for anyone else. The more I rehearse what God has already done, the more encouraged I am to pursue what he's yet to do.

After you write a few of these stories, please feel free to send them my way at edward@themovement.church. I want to be encouraged by how God is moving in your ministry as well.

If there is anything I can do to serve and support you and your ministry, please don't hesitate to reach out. This road is better traveled together.

To believers. If God is at work in your church, then stay, serve, commit, give, and go all in. There is too much work to be done for you to be on the sidelines. When you give your local church your best, then in addition to honoring God with your efforts, you are also a tremendous blessing to your pastor.

If God isn't at work in your church, do something about it. Either be part of revitalizing your community of faith or get out of there. There's too much work to be done to be part of a church that isn't willing to do whatever it takes to keep reaching people with the gospel.

To unbelievers. I encourage you to place your faith in Jesus Christ for the forgiveness of your sins. In an instant, you will receive Christ's mercy and grace, and you will be made right with God forever. Then join a church committed to bringing the life-changing message of Jesus Christ to the ends of the earth. Only God can give you what you are longing for.

Afterword

Many years ago, while ministering in Brazil, I picked up a proverb that I've recited often. "The heart cannot taste what the eyes have not seen." Recently, my eyes saw and my heart tasted of the great grace of Christ among the people of THEMOVEMENT.CHURCH. While speaking and leading prayer at this young congregation's very first all-church retreat, my wife and I saw, sensed, and celebrated the fruit of all you have just experienced as you've read Edward's recounting of God's unique work in and through his people.

As you've been inspired by Edward's recounting of the works of God, I hope you will remember that the Lord is not obligated to miraculous reruns, but he is committed to magnificent revelations of his character. The beauty of this book is not that it inspires you to expect God to work in your life the same way he worked in these stories. Rather, Edward points us to the character of God. Our unchanging Lord is ready to reveal himself to you today to transform your life, family, ministry, and work. *Only God* inspires us all to remember these things:

God redeems those who fail him. Maybe you are over-zealous in pursuing your own goals, like the younger version of Edward. Perhaps you've contributed to some stress fractures in your closest relationships. You may have allowed sin and rebellion to wreck your life, as so many of those reached by THEMOVEMENT.CHURCH did. Regardless of your mistakes, remember that *only God* can make all things new by the power of his gospel of grace.

God rewards those who seek him. Having journeyed with Edward in our growth in prayer, I can attest, as he has, that "Without faith it is impossible to please him, for whoever would draw near to God must believe that he exists and that he rewards those who seek him" (Heb. 11:6). The story of THEMOVEMENT.CHURCH is a story of the pleasure of God in response to believing, risk-taking, gospel-centered prayer. I hope that as you have read the accounts of Edward's journey, your heart is motivated like never before to draw near to God, with full confidence in his glorious character. Seek *him*—not just his hand but his face. As you call on the Lord in earnest faith, you will be able to trust his hand to do what is best in your life for his glory and for the sake of the gospel through your ministry efforts, whatever they may be.

God reconciles those who trust him. *Only God* is not a whitewashed story about perfect interpersonal dynamics. You've read about the tensions of ministry relationships, the challenges of connecting to unbelieving community leaders, and the often overwhelming task of communicating God's love to people far away from God. Yet woven throughout the stories of this church is the beautiful thread of the reconciling grace of the gospel. As I reflect on the journey of THEMOVEMENT.CHURCH, I am drawn once again to the truths of 2 Corinthians 5:18–21:

Afterword

All this is from God, who through Christ reconciled us to himself and gave us the ministry of reconciliation; that is, in Christ God was reconciling the world to himself, not counting their trespasses against them, and entrusting to us the message of reconciliation. Therefore, we are ambassadors for Christ, God making his appeal through us. We implore you on behalf of Christ, be reconciled to God. For our sake he made him to be sin who knew no sin, so that in him we might become the righteousness of God.

As you turn the final pages of this book, I hope you will know the movement of God in *your* life. Sense his movement toward you to reconcile your heart to his. Obey *his* movement in you to compel you to seek reconciliation in every relationship. Trust *his* movement through you as his ambassador of reconciliation. It may not be in Oakland, but the needs and opportunities are paramount everywhere. Whether it is Oklahoma, Omaha, Orange County, Orlando, or somewhere overseas, I know it is Edward's prayer that you will trust our great Christ to make his appeal through you. "Be reconciled to God."

Daniel Henderson
President, Strategic Renewal International
www.strategicrenewal.com

Acknowledgments

To my wife, Rebekah. Thank you for reflecting the steadfast love of Christ through your steadfast love for me. Your patience with me is a gift I do not deserve. I love you.

To the original Core Team. Rebekah, Josh, Sarah, Chanthan, Stacey, Spencer, Lanae, Chadd, Cheryl, Ashley, Quinton, Alicia, Danny, Christina, Rich, Rhonda, Eryn, Jenny, and Randy—although all our relationships may not be what they once were, I will never take for granted the years we shared together. The church that exists today and the impact it is having in the city of Oakland would not be possible without the tremendous amount of faith, sacrifice, and hard work you invested in those early years. Thank you.

To First Baptist Church in Trussville, Alabama, and Redeemer Baptist Church in Paso Robles, California. Thank you for the specific financial contributions you made to make the publishing of this book a reality. I pray that God honors your faith to believe that this project was good soil for your resources.

To Lucid Books. Thank you for taking a risk on a new, unestablished writer. The story of the miracles God performed in and through our church does not have the opportunity to be told in this form if you don't first believe it is a story worth telling. Thank you.

Appendix 1

30 Attributes of God

1 – God Is a Resurrector

Only God can bring life from death.

2 – God Is a Promoter

Only God can gift you opportunities that your lack of education and experience should disqualify you from.

3 – God Is a Burden-Giver

Only God can burden your heart for the things that break his heart.

4 – God Is a Unifier

Only God can develop relational unity around a calling that will require that the relationship pay a price.

5 – God Is an Equipper

Only God can call people who are overqualified to follow you to commit to your vision.

6 – God Is a Provider

Only God can prepare and position people you don't know to bring financial provision into your vision.

7 – God Is a Prayer-Answerer

Only God can answer your prayers supernaturally.

8 – God Is a Door-Opener

Only God can position you to be received where most are rejected.

9 – God Is a Rescuer

Only God can save a soul.

10 – God Is a Pruner

Only God can employ subtraction as a means of multiplication.

11 – God Is a Labor-Sender

Only God can send people to help you rebuild that which the enemy tried to destroy.

12 – God Is a Convictor

Only God can convict someone to choose him over the pleasures and comforts of the world.

13 – God Is a Border-Enlarger

Only God can extend your impact in ways you never expected.

14 – God Is a Humbler

Only God can replace a spirit of entitlement with a posture of humility.

15 – God Is a Commission-Giver

Only God can command that the local church repent of its misprioritization and return to his original mandate to go and make disciples.

16 – God Is a Restorer
Only God can use a downturn to be the setup for an upgrade.

17 – God Is a Way-Maker
Only God can leverage our failures as the way to accomplish his purposes.

18 – God Is a Reviver
Only God can break through the routine of faith to bring revival to your faith.

19 – God Is a Reconciler
Only God can require repentance within a team to reconcile relationships on a team.

20 – God Is a Father
Only God can discern between the wants and needs of his children and decide when we should be given either.

21 – God Is Holy
Only God can reveal that the ultimate purpose of praying to God is worshipping God.

22 – God Is a Guider
Only God can direct the steps that getting to his destination demands.

23 – God Is a Dream-Giver
Only God can inspire you to wholeheartedly pursue dreams that cannot be accomplished unless his power is present.

24 – God Is a Healer
Only God can administer healing to our pains for which there is no earthly cure.

25 – God Is a Blesser

Only God can bless you through the people he chooses to love you.

26 – God Is a Helper

Only God can help you beyond the ways you expect him to uphold you.

27 – God Is a Knitter

Only God can knit together the type of team the world couldn't keep together.

28 – God Is a Sanctifier

Only God can assign the mundane as a means of making someone into his masterpiece.

29 – God Is a Redeemer

Only God can create beauty from ashes.

30 – God Is a Wounder

Only God can wound you to bless you.

Appendix 2

The Church I See

Passionately Proclaims the Gospel

The church I see is focused first on passionately proclaiming the good news that God saves sinners. The church I see labors tirelessly to clearly, creatively, and compellingly communicate that salvation comes by grace alone, through faith alone, in Christ alone. Every event, program, initiative, partnership, and endeavor the church pursues is motivated by the gospel. The church I see reaches people with the gospel, renews people by the gospel, and releases people for the gospel.

Relentlessly Reaches the Lost

The primary aim of our gospel proclamation is to reach people who do not yet have a relationship with Jesus Christ. The church I see is unapologetically aware of and sensitive to the needs of those who have never been part of a church and those who have been hurt or disillusioned by the church. Because lost people matter to God most, the church I see does anything and everything short of sin to build bridges to and make connections with people who are far from Christ.

Deliberately Develops Disciples

The church I see is not satisfied with just seeing people get saved. The church I see is committed to intentionally developing fully devoted followers of Jesus Christ who make fully devoted followers of Jesus Christ. The church I see makes disciples who make disciples. The church I see measures its success not by how many people are attending its services but by how many people are turning from their selfish ways and picking up their cross to follow Jesus.

Strategically Serves the City

As a community of faith filled with fully devoted followers of Jesus Christ, the church I see seeks to bring shalom to its city. The church I see makes itself aware of the needs within the city and develops strategic partnerships and alliances to see those needs met. The church I see gives specific attention to the poor, the widows, and the orphans. As a result of its commitment to the well-being of the city, the church I see is a church that the city—believers and nonbelievers alike—absolutely loves.

Methodically Multiplies Itself

Because the church I see develops disciples who are released for the gospel, the church I see multiplies. Because the need is so great, the church I see multiplies in the city, in the county, in the state, in the nation, and eventually around the world. The church I see plants churches that plant churches that plant churches. The church I see sends people who send people who send people. The church I see reaches the nations with the gospel of Jesus Christ.

Appendix 3

Our Discipleship Process

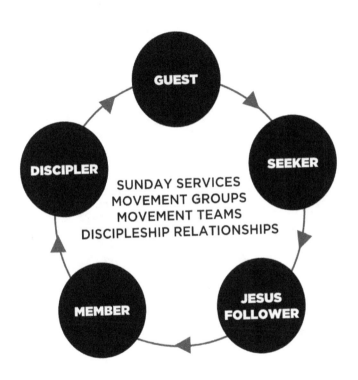

Appendix 4

Our 1–1 Discipleship Tools

FOR YOUR LEADING
What you need to KNOW

The Mandate for Our Mission — The Great Commission

Then Jesus came to them and said, "All authority in heaven and on earth has been given to me. Therefore go and make disciples of all nations, baptizing them in the name of the Father and of the Son and of the Holy Spirit, and teaching them to obey everything I have commanded you. And surely I am with you always, to the very end of the age."
MATTHEW 28:19-21

DISCIPLESHIP IS A COMMAND
"Therefore go and make disciples..."

BAPTIZING AND TEACHING IS THE WAY
"baptizing them...and teaching them..."

JESUS IS WITH YOU
"And surely I am with you..."

EVERYONE MUST BE DISCIPLED
"...go and make disciples of all nations..."

OBEDIENCE TO JESUS IS THE RESULT
"teaching them to obey everything I have commanded..."

JESUS IS WITH YOU FOREVER
"...always, to the very end of the age..."

The Model for Our Movement — Multiplication

You then, my son, be strong in the grace that is in Christ Jesus. And the things you have heard me say in the presence of many witnesses entrust to reliable people who will also be qualified to teach others.
2 TIMOTHY 2:1-2

PAUL → TIMOTHY → RELIABLE PEOPLE → TEACH OTHERS

"...the things you have heard me say..."   "...entrust to reliable people..."   "...who will...teach others..."

The Marker for Our Maturity — Christ-Like Love for One Another

"A new command I give you: Love one another. **As I have loved you, so you must love one another.**
By this everyone will know that you are my disciples, if you love one another."
JOHN 13:34-35

FOR THE MEETING
What you need to DO

7 Stories of Hope

The Sinful Woman - Luke 7:36-50
Who Can Come to God? - Luke 18:9-17
God Forgives - Matthew 18:21-35
The Cost of Following Christ - Matthew 16:21-28
The Death of Jesus - Luke 22:66-23:25; 23:32-43
Jesus Is Alive - Luke 24:1-20; 36-53
Merciful Father - Luke 15:11-32

8 Commands of Christ

Repent and Believe (Mark 1:15) - Luke 19:1-10
Be Baptized (Matthew 28:19) - Acts 8:26-39
Pray (Matthew 6:9-13) - Matthew 6:5-15
Go...Make Disciples (Matthew 28:19-20) - John 4:4-42
Love (Matthew 22:37-39) - Luke 10:25-37
Commemorate Jesus' Death (Luke 22:19-20) - Luke 22:7-20
Give (Luke 6:38) - Mark 12:41-44
Meet Together (Hebrews 10:24-25) - Acts 2:41-47

3 Discipleship Musts

READ TOGETHER - Read Scriptures Aloud
What does this say about God/Jesus? Say about me?

OBEY TOGETHER - Identify Steps of Obedience
What is the last thing God told you to do?

PRAY TOGETHER - Pray Aloud
What is the corporate prayer we're feeling led to pray?

10 Corporate Prayers

UPROOT SIN
John 15:1-2 | Romans 8:9-14

SUPPLY NEEDS
Matthew 6:11 | Philippians 4:18-19

RENEW OAKLAND
Isaiah 62:6-7 | Jeremiah 29:7

SPIRIT FALL
Acts 2:1-4 | Acts 11:15-16

BURDEN HEARTS
Nehemiah 1:3-4 | Romans 9:1-3

ENLARGE TERRITORY
1 Chronicles 4:10 | Acts 1:8

SAVE SOULS
1 Timothy 2:1-4 | 2 Peter 3:9

SEND LABORERS
Matthew 9:37-38 | Romans 10:14-15

INCREASE AWE
Proverbs 9:10 | Isaiah 6:1-6

GUARD UNITY
Psalm 133:1-3 | John 17:21

AFTER THE FIRST 15
What we recommend you READ

13 Meetings Reading the Book of James

MEETING 16 - James 1:1 ; John 15:20
MEETING 17 - James 1:2-18; Acts 11:26
MEETING 18 - James 1:19-27; Luke 9:23
MEETING 19 - James 2:1-13; James 1:17; James 1:27
MEETING 20 - James 2:14-26; Luke 10:25-37
MEETING 21 - James 3:1-12; Ephesians 5:4
MEETING 22 - James 3:13-18; James 1:22; James 2:14-26
MEETING 23 - James 4:1-12
MEETING 24 - James 4:13-17
MEETING 25 - James 5:1-6; Matthew 6:19-21
MEETING 26 - James 5:7-12; Mark 13:32; Acts 4:1-11; 1 Thessalonians 4:13-18; 1 Thessalonians 5:1-11
MEETING 27 - James 5:13-18
MEETING 28 - James 5:19-20; Genesis 3:8-9; Matthew 1:23

3 Impactful Discipleship Questions

DISCERNMENT QUESTION - *What is God saying to you through this?*
OBEDIENCE QUESTION - *What are you going to do about it?*
SUPPORT QUESTION - *What can I do to help?*

GOING DEEPER

More questions you can ASK

17 Personal-Accountability Questions

1. How are you consciously or unconsciously creating the impression that you are better than you really are? In what ways are you a hypocrite?
2. Have you been honest in all your acts and words, or do you exaggerate?
3. Do you confidentially pass onto another what was told you in confidence?
4. How are you a slave to dress, friends, work, or habits?
5. How are you self-conscious, self-pitying, or self-justifying, or prideful?
6. Have you given the Bible time to speak to you?
7. How are you enjoying prayer?
8. What do you find yourself grumbling and complaining about?
9. Do you pray about the money you spend?
10. Have you been jealous, impure, critical, irritable, touchy, or distrustful?
11. Have you disobeyed God in anything?
12. Are you insisting on doing something that your conscience is uneasy about?
13. Are you feeling defeated in any part of your life?
14. How do you spend your spare time?
15. Do you thank God that you are not like other people? Like the Pharisee who despised the publican?
16. Is there anyone whom you fear, dislike, disown, criticize, hold resentment toward, or disregard? If so, what are you going to do about it?
17. How has Christ been real to you?

7 Evangelism Questions

1. When did you last speak to someone about your faith?
2. Who is an unbeliever who you are intentionally growing in relationship with?
3. Who was the last person you invited to church?
4. Who is the next person you will invite to church?
5. Whose salvation are you consistently praying for?
6. How are you positioning yourself to have relationships with non-believers?
7. How strong is your desire to reach the lost?

Appendix 5

The Leadership Team I See

Laughs Together

We laugh. We laugh at ourselves. We laugh at each other. We laugh at our mistakes. We laugh at our circumstances. We will take God and the mission of the church very seriously, but we will not take ourselves too seriously. And if we find ourselves short on things to laugh about, we will always take time to laugh at the absurdity that God actually chose us to lead his church.

Leads Together

We lead. We are not yes-men and yes-women. We take initiative in our roles and do not wait to be told what to do. We lead ourselves. We lead our teams. We lead the church. We are extremely aware of the fact that the health and strength of the church rise and fall on the health and strength of our leadership.

Listens Together

We listen. We listen to God. We listen to each other. We listen to our members. We listen to our guests. We listen to the community. We understand that we can learn more about each other and the people we've been called to serve by listening. We understand that we can meet needs best by listening. We understand that we can avoid and resolve conflict and frustration by listening. We understand that if we don't listen, someone else will, and opportunities will be lost.

Learns Together

We learn. We learn from the scriptures. We learn from other churches. We learn from each other. We learn from people both inside and outside of the church. We learn from both our fans and our critics. We learn from conferences, books, podcasts, vodcasts, blogs, vlogs, and mentors. We have an ever-increasing appetite for learning because we understand that not all learners are leaders, but all leaders are learners.

Lasts Together

We last. We last through ups and downs. We last through good times and bad. We last through triumphs and transitions. We understand that every great team and every great organization has at its foundation a group of people who have committed to last. We understand that for our mission of overwhelming Oakland with love to become a reality, longevity must become a necessity.

Appendix 6

Our 10 Corporate Prayers

1 – Uproot Sin
He cuts off every branch of mine that doesn't produce fruit, and he prunes the branches that do bear fruit so they will produce even more (John 15:2 NLT).

2 – Increase Awe
Fear of the LORD is the foundation of wisdom. Knowledge of the Holy One results in good judgment (Prov. 9:10 NLT).

3 – Save Souls
I urge you, first of all, to pray for all people. Ask God to help them; intercede on their behalf, and give thanks for them. This is good and pleases God our Savior, who wants everyone to be saved and to understand the truth (1 Tim. 2:1, 3–4 NLT).

4 – Renew Oakland
And work for the peace and prosperity of the city where I sent you into exile. Pray to the LORD for it, for its welfare will determine your welfare (Jer. 29:7 NLT).

5 – Enlarge Territory
"Oh, that you would bless me and expand my territory! Please be with me in all that I do, and keep me from all trouble and pain!" And God granted him his request (1 Chron. 4:10 NLT).

6 – Burden Hearts

"The wall of Jerusalem has been torn down, and the gates have been destroyed by fire." When I heard this, I sat down and wept. In fact, for days I mourned, fasted, and prayed to the God of heaven (Neh. 1:3–4 NLT).

7 – Spirit Fall

"As I began to speak," Peter continued, "the Holy Spirit fell on them, just as he fell on us at the beginning. Then I thought of the Lord's words when he said, 'John baptized with water, but you will be baptized with the Holy Spirit'" (Acts 11:15–16 NLT).

8 – Supply Needs

And this same God who takes care of me will supply all your needs from his glorious riches, which have been given to us in Christ Jesus (Phil. 4:19 NLT).

9 – Guard Unity

I pray that they will all be one, just as you and I are one—as you are in me, Father, and I am in you. And may they be in us so that the world will believe you sent me (John 17:21 NLT).

10 – Send Laborers

He said to his disciples, "The harvest is great, but the workers are few. So pray to the Lord who is in charge of the harvest; ask him to send more workers into his fields" (Matt. 9:37–38 NLT).

Appendix 7

The Corporate Prayer Culture I See

Humble

God resists the proud but gives grace to the humble. The corporate prayer culture I see is humble. We pray humbly. We praise humbly. We petition humbly. We are speaking to the King of kings and Lord of lords. We pray humbly because it is only by grace that we have received Jesus Christ who gives us access to God. We pray humbly because we are aware that everything from the breath in our lungs to the galaxies in the sky are created and controlled by the God to whom we pray.

Accessible

We should not make it difficult for people who are turning to God. The corporate prayer culture I see is accessible to non-Christians, new Christians, and mature saints. We will make corporate prayer something everyone can involve themselves in regardless of where they are on their spiritual journey. We will keep corporate prayer accessible by not only explaining what we are doing but also why we are doing it. Success in prayer will be measured not only by how we are praying but also by the number of inexperienced people who catch on and participate in corporate prayer.

Biblical

If you abide in me, and my words abide in you, ask whatever you wish, and it will be done for you. The corporate prayer culture I see is biblical. We pray the scriptures. We praise God with the scriptures. We petition God with the scriptures. Praying biblically gives us confidence as we pray, it gives us accuracy as we pray, it gives us balance as we pray, and it gives us truth as we pray. We pray biblically because we believe it is best to talk to God using God's Word. We pray biblically because in doing so, we teach people that anyone can pray.

Faith-Full

It is impossible to please God without faith. The corporate prayer culture I see is full of faith—faith in God's love, goodness, and wisdom. Our prayers are full of faith because our God is full of power. We will pray faith-filled prayers not to move God's hands but to change our hearts. We will exemplify faith-filled prayer by asking until we receive, seeking until we find, and knocking until doors are opened. The fullness of our faith will most clearly be represented by the posture of our hearts in prayer, which declares in every prayer, "Nevertheless, not my will, but your will be done."

Multipliable

"But the word of the Lord continued to grow and to be multiplied" (Acts 12:24 NASB). The corporate prayer culture I see is multipliable. Because we pray humbly, accessibly, biblically, and full of faith, corporate prayer spreads throughout our Sunday services, our discipleship relationships, our groups, our volunteer teams, and ultimately our family of churches. Because our culture of corporate prayer is multipliable, we will be known not as a church that prays but as a praying church!

Appendix 8

The Financial Stewardship I See

Vision-Driven Spending
How much does the vision require us to invest?

We will not allow our financial resources to determine the size of our vision. Instead, the size and scope of our vision will determine the amount of financial resources we will trust God to provide. If it's God's will, it's God's bill. What the King wants, the King pays for. If the vision God has given us requires it, we will invest in it. If given the option between vision-driven spending and fear-driven saving, we will choose investing in the vision every single time.

Stewardship-Inspired Responsibility
Are we ready to answer to God for this allocation of resources?

We will be held accountable for every penny. God has his eyes on every dollar that comes in and every dollar that goes out, and there will be a day when we will answer to God for the financial resources he allowed to come through our hands. We are not owners; we are stewards. We will be responsible with our finances with the understanding that they are ultimately God's. This understanding of stewardship will drive both our prudent restraint and our faith-filled risk.

Grace-Guided Generosity
How much does grace compel us to give?

We will be generous with compensation. We will be generous with appreciation. We will be generous with benevolence. We will be generous with partnerships. We will be generous with missions. We will be generous in unexpected circumstances. We will be generous even if it puts us in an uncomfortable financial situation. In every occasion, we will be as generous with our finances toward others as God has been generous with his grace toward us.

Trust-Building Transparency
If this expenditure was made public, would it increase trust or erode it?

We will not hide anything because there will be nothing to hide. In a world where faith in religious institutions and religious leaders to manage financial resources is extremely low, we will be the exception to the rule. Before our pastors, staff, members, the IRS, and a watching world, we will be open, honest, and transparent about all our financial dealings. We will take every measure possible to ensure that every number on our balance sheet is accurate and that we'd be proud to share it!

Appendix 9

The Pastoral Team I See

Leads Together

The pastoral team I see leads together. We gather a sense of where God is leading, and we lead our church in the same direction. The pastoral team I see leads with faith, conviction, and boldness. The pastoral team I see is convinced that the height, depth, and width of our faith-filled leadership decisions will determine the height, depth, and width of the faith of those who call THEMOVEMENT.CHURCH home. The pastoral team I see is unified in our leadership, and we refuse to move forward on a decision or in a direction until we all have a sense of peace and rightness about where we believe the Lord is leading our church community.

Shepherds Together

The pastoral team I see shepherds together. We understand that no one pastor can singlehandedly care for the needs of the entire flock. The pastoral team I see invests their time with the individuals and families within the congregation so the team has a strong handle on how the majority of our community members are doing with their personal walks with the Lord. The pastoral team I see shepherds toward obedience in every area of a person's life, and we do so with grace and with truth. If given the choice between speaking the truth and being liked, the pastoral team I see speaks truth *every single time*. The pastoral team I see also shepherds each other, giving special attention to the health of the lead pastor.

Teaches Together

The pastoral team I see teaches together. We buy in wholeheartedly to the truth that the proclaimed Word of God is central to the health of the church and that the responsibility for that teaching lies squarely on our shoulders. The pastoral team I see is united around what is taught and how it is taught. The pastoral team I see is aware of the spiritual needs of the congregation and ensures that many of those needs are being met in the pulpit. The teaching of the pastoral team I see is characterized by a sensitivity to those who are far from Christ and an emphasis on the finished work of Christ as the power for salvation.

Prays Together

The pastoral team I see prays together. We know that apart from the power and presence of God, what we are endeavoring to accomplish is impossible. The pastoral team I see is simultaneously humbled by the enormous task yet hopeful and reliant on the Holy Spirit to empower us for every good work he calls us to. The pastoral team I see adds fasting to our prayer because we are hungrier for God's power than we are for our comfort. The pastoral team I see prays for the will of God, for the miracles of God, and for the vision God has given us until it comes to pass.

Appendix 10

Our Primary Guiding Document

Our Mission – *Why do we exist?*
Overwhelm Oakland with love.

Our Vision – *Where are we headed?*
We are a movement of disciples making disciples who plant churches who plant churches.

Our Strategy – *What do we do?*
1. Sunday Services
2. Community Groups
3. Volunteer Teams
4. 1–1 Discipleship Relationships

Our Values – *How do we behave?*
1. Lifelong Learning (Growth > Complacency)
2. Audacious Faith (Courage > Comfort)
3. Selfless Transparency (Truth Telling > Image Protecting)
4. Empowering Leadership (Development > Excellence)
5. Resolute Gratitude (Thanksgiving > Entitlement)

Our Dream – *What is our big, hairy, audacious goal?*
By 2026, we will be a family of eight churches meeting in eight public schools in Oakland, serving eight faculties, eight student bodies, and eight neighborhoods.